New York, N. Y. 10027

ISRAEL AFTER BEGIN

Books by Daniel Gavron

The End of Days (novel)
Walking Through Israel
Israel After Begin

ISRAEL AFTER BEGIN

*Israel's Options in the
Aftermath of the Lebanon War*

Daniel Gavron

WITHDRAWN

Boston
Houghton Mifflin Company
1984

Bur
DS
126.5
·G36
1984
copy 1

Copyright © 1984 by Daniel Gavron

All rights reserved. No part of this work may be reproduced
or transmitted in any form or by any means, electronic or
mechanical, including photocopying and recording, or by
any information storage or retrieval system, except as
may be expressly permitted by the 1976 Copyright Act or in
writing from the publisher. Requests for permission should
be addressed in writing to Houghton Mifflin Company,
2 Park Street, Boston, Massachusetts 02108.

Library of Congress Cataloging in Publication Data

Gavron, Daniel.
  Israel after Begin.

  1. Israel—Politics and government. 2. Lebanon—History—Israeli in-
tervention, 1982–   . 3. Begin, Menachem, 1913–   . 4. Jews,
Oriental—Israel. 5. Jewish–Arab relations—1973–   . 6. Israel—Eth-
nic relations. I. Title.
DS126.5.G36   1984   956.94'053   83-22650
ISBN 0-395-35320-3

Printed in the United States of America

S 10 9 8 7 6 5 4 3 2 1

mpk 1984·12.3 — 117461

For
Etan, Ilana, Assaf
my children
with hope for a better world

Contents

ISRAEL AFTER BEGIN

1
The New-Style War

"The Israel that we saw here yesterday is not the Israel we have seen in the past. The stench of terror was all across the city. Nothing like it has ever happened in this part of the world. I kept thinking yesterday of the bombing of Madrid in the Spanish civil war. What in the world is going on? Israel's security problem on its border is fifty miles to the south. What is the Israeli army doing here in Beirut? The answer is that we are now dealing with an imperial Israel, which is solving its problems in someone else's city — world opinion be damned."

That commentary — *diatribe* is perhaps a better word — was delivered by NBC's John Chancellor in Beirut on August 3, 1982, as the Israeli invasion of Lebanon was about to enter its third month.

Chancellor was standing within walking distance of the former Palestinian neighborhood of Tel Zaatar, reduced to ruins amid horrible carnage just six years earlier. Media reports at the time spoke of at least two thousand dead bodies and described how the Christian Lebanese looters had to cover their faces with handkerchiefs against the stench.

The eminent commentator was standing in the Lebanese capital, an intermittent battleground for seven years. According to Lebanese estimates, some ninety thousand people had been killed in the civil war before the Israelis came. As early as 1976, Ghassan Tueni, the Lebanese information minister, told reporters in Geneva that the casualty toll for the war was sixty thousand dead and two hundred thousand wounded.

The Palestine Liberation Organization (PLO) set up its headquarters in Beirut after it was expelled from the Kingdom of Jordan in September 1970, still called by the Palestinians Black September, in memory of the thousands slaughtered in the Jordanian camps by King Hussein's Arab Legion.

"Nothing like it has ever happened in this part of the world," pronounced Chancellor, justifying the claim of many Israelis that "the whole world is against us." If only Chancellor's hyperbole had been an isolated instance; but it was not.

U.S. Colonel Trevor N. Depuy, author of some eighty books on military affairs, spent five hours observing the bombing of Beirut on August 12 and estimated that "during that time no more than one hundred fifty bombs were dropped on Beirut." The *Washington Post* reported the following day that sixteen hundred bombs had been dropped, which, Depuy said, "suggested an intensity of at least four times greater than what I saw." That same day the *International Herald Tribune* reported (without comment) the PLO contention that forty-two thousand bombs had been dropped.

There were also reports of "the destruction of Tyre and Sidon," and many more instances of exaggerations and distortions in the Western media, which made it difficult for Israelis like me to take a critical stand against our own government, for at times it does indeed seem as if the whole world is against us.

However, espousing the statement of a lieutenant colonel in the Israel Defense Forces that "it is our actions which harm us — not what others write about those actions," I have decided to take Chancellor seriously. Let us then ignore the hyperbole and agree that this "is not the Israel we have seen in the past." Let us also consider his question, "What in the world is going on?"

I imagine myself in a room far from Jerusalem, where I live, with about a dozen Americans and Europeans. They are not hostile to Israel, I postulate, but they are deeply disturbed by what happened in Lebanon and by what is happening on the West Bank. They are saying, "Look, you grew up in our cultural tradition, but you have lived in Israel for two decades. You have served in the Israeli army and your son has just returned from service in Lebanon. What the devil is going on there?" I smile and give a very Israeli shrug of the shoulders, to indicate that I am confused myself and that I don't really know either. But they persist, "If you can't explain it, then who the hell can?"

And I take a deep breath because I know just who can. Our implacable enemies — those who obscenely compare us with the Nazis — can. They will be only too pleased to explain. So will our own superpatriots, those Israelis who believe we can do no wrong. If I continue to smile and shrug my shoulders, I will leave the field clear for the anti-Semites or the paranoid Jews. That would be a shame, for we are neither ape nor angel, but, like most peoples, something in between. That is much harder to explain, of course, but I will not hide behind complexity. If we moderates will not speak out clearly, the extremists deserve to win. So I am going to explain the situation in all its subtlety, but I am going to tell it straight.

First off, this was not an unprovoked Israeli attack. It is true that there was a cease-fire in the north, which held for a year before the war, but the PLO was building an impressive military infrastructure and could have launched hit-and-run attacks at any time.

In 1978 the Israelis pushed the PLO out of South Lebanon in Operation Litani, but two years later they were back, launching their terrorist raids. In May 1980 I arrived at Misgav Am, high up in the hills of Galilee, minutes after the killing of a five-man PLO gang, which had invaded the kibbutz the previous night. Before the invaders had been wiped out by an elite Israel Defense Forces (IDF) unit, they had managed to kill a soldier, a civilian, and a two-year-old boy.

Their target had been the kibbutz baby house — in some communal settlements the children sleep apart from their parents. They had captured the building without difficulty, holding the six babies and their adult guard hostage against demands to free PLO prisoners held in Israeli jails. That morning the IDF soldiers had taken the house by storm.

It was a horrific sight: fresh blood was still spattered on the walls and tiled floor. Smashed furniture and ripped mattresses were scattered around. A headless doll lay next to a limbless teddy bear. Cots and cupboards had been overturned. Bullets had plowed into the plaster of the walls and even drilled holes in the metal stair rail. The broken glass crunched under my feet as I walked.

A number of kibbutz members wandered like zombies through the rubble, stunned by the destruction. The normally ebullient journalists conversed in low tones. Later, when I heard my own description of the scene on the radio, I could hardly recognize my own voice: cots and toys do not belong on a battlefield.

I met Ami Gluska of the army spokesman's office, who was later to become the personal assistant to President Yitzhak Navon. His fine, dark face was lined with grief as he explained that the two-year-old who had been killed was his nephew. His sister and her husband had been at Misgav Am for only a year, trying to decide whether kibbutz life suited them.

Outside the devastated building it was a peaceful Sabbath scene, with the sun shining down out of a clear blue sky on the well-tended lawns, the neat flower beds, the white houses with their red-tiled roofs. On the lawn outside the kibbutz dining hall sat the young soldiers who had stormed the baby house.

Khaki-clad, tousle-haired, wearing their brown paratroop boots, they looked about fourteen or fifteen years old — far too young for the business of killing. They were sober and not in the least triumphant, even when their commanding officer addressed them and praised their bravery. I searched the faces, looking for my own son, at that time a conscript in one of the elite units; he was not there.

Defense Minister Ezer Weizman had arrived with the chief of staff. The lanky Weizman, with his trim mustache and wiry graying hair, was always happy to crack jokes, but not this time. His face was grave as he crisply described the action and listed the casualties. He then spoke about morale.

"I am always amazed when I visit a kibbutz after one of these attacks," he told me. "I see my task as giving them courage to go on, but it is always they who strengthen me. I asked them what we could do to help and they asked me what they could do."

The adult killed in the attack had been the secretary of the kibbutz. His deputy, now acting secretary, spoke calmly. "We came here to build our lives in peace. We will continue to live here and to develop Galilee for the good of all its citizens. Nothing will ever divert us from this task."

It was different the following year, when I drove up to Kiryat Shmona, a town populated for the most part by immigrants to Israel in the 1950s. Under continuous bombardment from PLO artillery and *katyusha* (Russian-made) rockets, most of the sixteen thousand population had fled southward.

Around Lake Kinneret, the Sea of Galilee, twenty miles to the south, it was still peaceful enough. Vacationers were sipping iced drinks in the lakeside cafés and the water-skiers were out in force. In nearby kibbutzim, mothers were pushing prams and fathers were playing with their children on the lawns. The scene was one of pastoral tranquillity.

A few miles north lay a different country: the blackened hillsides were burning and the acrid smell filled my nostrils. The boom of the distant artillery never ceased. I drove through the deserted streets of Kiryat Shmona and joined a frightened group of women and children who were spending their seventh successive day underground. It was stifling in the shelter.

A smiling girl soldier was strumming a guitar and leading them all in songs of peace. The young voices sang with fervor, and I blinked back the tears as I joined in.

That was in 1981, a year before the war. A cease-fire had been worked out through the good offices of the United States, but the PLO had won a sort of victory. It was not the Israeli bombing and shelling that stopped them. Only after the cease-fire was the majority of citizens able to return home and the minority who had remained to emerge from the shelters into the fresh air. If Misgav Am had proved that the PLO could never hope to take an inch of Galilee, Kiryat Shmona had demonstrated its ability to make normal life impossible for many of Israel's northern settlements.

So despite the fact that there had been no katyusha rockets or artillery shells for a year, the PLO did have a sword of Damocles hanging over Galilee, and most of us felt it was an intolerable situation. When the initial IDF thrust into Lebanon came, most Israelis greeted it with a sigh of relief.

We thought that we were embarking on a forty-eight-hour operation, a repeat of the Litani operation, to kick the PLO out of range once more. Many wondered whether there was any point in repeating the performance every four or five years. Some of us asked ourselves whether such methods could ever lead to a permanent solution of the problem; no one imagined that we had embarked on a full-scale war that was to last more than a year.

Prime Minister Menachem Begin and Defense Minister Ariel Sharon had in fact initiated an ambitious scheme to solve the Palestinian problem by force. Sharon's plan was to destroy the Palestinian national movement by smashing the PLO once and for all and to link up with the Christian Phalangists to create a "new order" in Lebanon. It was not the sort of action that could have been launched by "the Israel we have seen." Consequently, it was some time before we realized what was happening.

All Israel's previous wars had been defensive in nature, with the possible exception of the Sinai Campaign of 1956, and that was in essence a large-scale reprisal raid for terrorist attacks. In 1948 the newly proclaimed state was invaded by five Arab armies, which were pledged to wipe it out. In 1967 Israel launched an attack, but only after Egypt had closed the sea approaches to the

southern port of Elat, moved a large army into Sinai, and signed
pacts with Syria and Jordan. In 1973 Syria and Egypt took Israel
by surprise, attacking on the Day of Atonement, when much of
the country was at prayer. In 1978 Israel pushed the PLO out of
range and then withdrew.

In 1982, for the first time, Israel initiated a war, bombed and
shelled heavily populated areas, invaded an Arab capital, and
intervened in the affairs of a neighboring state. It was indeed
"not the Israel we have seen in the past."

Most of the Israeli cabinet did not even know what was envisaged. Prime Minister Begin told the Knesset, Israel's parliament
(and also wrote to President Reagan), that the aim was merely
to push the PLO back some forty-five kilometers, out of range of
the northern settlements.

Asher Walfish of the English-language *Jerusalem Post* first
reported how Sharon and Begin won the approval of their cabinet
colleagues. The cabinet, wrote Walfish, never had a proper discussion on the objectives of the campaign. Prime Minister Begin
and Sharon would seek approval for only one move at a time.
They did not explain the implications of these moves. Walfish
quotes an unnamed cabinet minister as telling him, "Some of us
felt that Sharon was keeping the implications to himself and his
aims, too, while merely asking us to approve 'a single chess move.'
As civilians we were like clay in the hands of the military man."

When one of the ministers, Yitzhak Berman, asked whether
the advances of each day's fighting would have to be secured on
the next day, Sharon "laughed like a child caught red-handed
raiding the larder." Asked whether it was the IDF plan to link
up with the Phalangists, thus influencing the forthcoming elections in Lebanon, Sharon said he had no intention of linking up
with them.

When Simha Ehrlich, the late deputy prime minister, and others gave media interviews on the anniversary of the war, they
served only to confirm Walfish's account. Even Sharon himself
acknowledged the truth of the report by implication, when he

said in an interview, "The sabotage did not start with the oppo-sition, but inside the cabinet itself in the first weeks of the war." These interviews aroused great interest in Israel, but, in fact, they added nothing important to what Walfish had already told us.

Later Walfish published an article explaining that the Sharon "grand design" had its origins in an old dream of the Revisionist Zionists, the precursors of Begin's Herut party. They believed in the idea of an Alliance of Minorities in the Middle East. They said that the Jews of Israel should ally themselves with the Copts of Egypt, the Maronite Christians of Lebanon, the Kurds of Iraq, the Druze of Syria, the Armenians, the Assyrians, the Turks, and the Persians against the Arab Muslim majority in the region.

The Labor movement, which controlled the pre-state Zionist movement and ruled Israel for its first three decades, rejected the concept as unrealistic. Israel did indeed make tactical alli-ances with Iran, Turkey, and Ethiopia, leapfrogging the sur-rounding enemy countries, but David Ben-Gurion, Israel's first prime minister, believed that Israel would ultimately have to come to terms with the Muslim Arabs. Labor governments extended aid to the Maronites in Lebanon and the Kurds in Iraq, but always with a considerable degree of discretion.

After 1976 the Israelis fostered the South Lebanon militias of Major Sa'ad Haddad and assisted the Christian Phalangists with arms and training, but there was never a plan for a full-scale alliance. This changed in 1977, shortly after Begin became prime minister. The young Phalangist commander, Bashir Jemayel, ruthlessly seized control of the other Christian militias, expand-ing his group into the Lebanese forces.

Apparently supported by the Mossad, Israel's general intelli-gence service (which had good connections with Jemayel), but against the advice of army intelligence (which had far wider contacts in Lebanon), Sharon "bought" a Phalangist plan to make Bashir Jemayel president of Lebanon and create a "new order," which would make peace with Israel and quell the Palestinians. The war was timed to precede the Lebanese presidential elec-tions, due in August.

Brigadier Binyamin Ben-Eliezer, the contact man with Jemayel (who has since disclosed that he frequently brought Jemayel, under the pseudonym Charlie, to his kibbutz), was quoted as saying that Israel and Lebanon would have signed a full-scale peace treaty if Bashir had lived; the evidence, however, points the other way.

As soon as he became president, Jemayel started distancing himself from Israel. Just a few days before his assassination, he was summoned to a "secret meeting" with Begin and Sharon and rebuked for his "ingratitude." But his policy was inevitable. The wealth and power of the Lebanese Christians is based on the Arab world. The Lebanese cannot afford to disengage from Saudi Arabia and the Gulf states. Israel fell into the trap set for it by the Phalangists, who were only too eager to get rid of Israel once the IDF had done the "dirty work."

Sharon's conception was unrealistic, but it was even more ambitious than the creation of a new order in Lebanon. Sharon wanted to smash the PLO and expel the Palestinian refugees from Lebanon (with Phalangist support) into Syria and thence to Jordan, where they could set up their Palestinian state.

Sharon is on record as supporting the idea that Israel should help the Palestinians to topple King Hussein and set up their state in Jordan.

This, then, was the grandiose scheme on which Israel, unknown to most of its government, Knesset, and population, embarked in June 1982. And that is what the Israeli army was doing in Beirut two months later. The country had been hijacked by a small group of men, but that realization came only gradually.

Although the Lebanon war, misnamed Operation Peace for Galilee, was still going on more than a year later, its active phase lasted only three months — from the time it was launched on June 6 until the PLO and the Syrians pulled out of Beirut on September 1.

Israel's ambassador to Britain, Shlomo Argov, was shot in the head on June 3. The following day Israel bombed twenty-two targets in Beirut and South Lebanon. On June 5, a Saturday, the

PLO fired hundreds of shells and rockets across the border. On June 6 the IDF drove into Lebanon, reaching the outskirts of Beirut in less than a week. On June 11 there was a cease-fire, which was broken the next day, and Israel pushed forward into Beirut. From June 21 to 25 there were fierce battles for control of the Beirut-Damascus road. By the end of the month, West Beirut was under siege.

For the next two months the IDF bombed and shelled West Beirut with varying degrees of intensity, while Philip Habib, the U.S. special ambassador, negotiated the withdrawal of the PLO and the Syrians. On August 23 Bashir Jemayel was elected president of Lebanon, and on September 1 the last PLO forces left the Lebanese capital. Sharon's grandiose plan had been implemented — or so it seemed at the time.

During those early weeks we were, above all, confused. We did not really know what we were being called on to support. Neither did we know what our consciences might require us to oppose.

At the outset we were, of course, swept along with the momentum. When Israel goes to war, the country moves into a different gear. It is then that you see us at our best: differences are forgotten and we all pull together, one big family, sharing its triumphs and mourning its losses.

The radio starts nonstop broadcasts of Israeli songs — songs of peace as well as military marches — interrupted by news flashes and bulletins. Soldiers waiting by the roadside are picked up immediately, and even the taxi drivers give free lifts. The volunteer organizations spring into action, and roadside stalls, offering free drinks and sandwiches, sprout like mushrooms after a spring rain.

The country's entertainment stars rush to the front to entertain the troops; Jewish public figures and well-wishers fly in from abroad. Israeli emigrants and vacationers jam the airlines and lay siege to the airports in an effort to get home.

In 1967 the poet Abba Kovner contrasted the way we go to war with that of other nations: "Their bayonets wreathed in gay flowers, their hobnailed boots crashing out the rhythm of the marching songs that swell from their throats . . . smiling and proud." In Israel it was different: "Never before have I seen a city rise so silently to the call of duty. This nation went to war filled with a sense of destiny, gravely and quietly prepared . . . This is my people, a people I did not know before."

This time, also, the soldiers, summoned by phone or broadcast call-up signs, moved quietly to their units, received their equipment, put on their uniforms, and reluctantly prepared to do their duty.

It was almost the same, but not quite. There was a sour taste in the mouth: the mobilization, the music, the bulletins — it had happened just a bit too often. We could not help wondering whether the government was exploiting the idealism and the patriotism for its own ends. This feeling had not yet crystallized for most of us, but it was there, even at the outset.

On a personal level I had a different problem: I had not been called up. Mobilized for the wars of 1967 and 1973, I had known the apprehension, the slightly self-conscious determination to do my duty, the moments of genuine fear. But the responsibility is taken out of your hands. Matters are beyond your control. You simply have to obey orders and this is a remarkably soothing feeling. Added to this is the fact that you are one of the "heroes," called to the colors to defend hearth and home.

Now, in 1982, I was cooling my heels and my son was in the thick of it. It was a terrible feeling. "Now you know what it's like," remarked my wife, not without satisfaction. I knew what she meant. Staying at home is far worse, and it is the perennial fate of the Israeli woman.

Watching the battles on television only made matters worse. Ze'ev, the brilliant cartoonist of the *Ha'aretz* newspaper, summed it up as only cartoonists can. He presented the war as an Atari television game. Begin, Sharon, Syrian President Hafez Assad,

PLO leader Yasir Arafat, and Philip Habib were pulling the levers and making explosions occur on a television screen. For those of us at home, the war was indeed a "television game."

By the fifth day I had become thoroughly fed up with playing it safe, and I drove north to do a story about the wounded in the Safad hospital. In Galilee I at last caught something of the ambience of war: the long convoys of military vehicles, the sweat-soaked, unshaven, khaki-clad soldiers, sipping their free drinks, the grease, the dust, the smell. The war was right there in Safad in the beautiful modern hospital. I stood on a veranda above the breathtaking sweep down toward Lake Kinneret and watched the heavy helicopters lumbering down from the north to settle with amazing lightness on the pad below.

The ambulances rushed their precious human cargo up the narrow road between the pad and the hospital, and the helicopters took off and nudged their way north to the battlefield. The roar of their engines punctuated my conversations.

The soldiers lay in the wards, their limbs, heads, or torsos bandaged. Some looked bloodless, they were so pale against the white sheets. Others sat up and managed a smile. Dr. Shimon Liberty circulated among his patients. A comfortable man, wearing a green surgical smock, he had a warm smile for everybody in his square, brown face.

Relaxing with a cigarette, Liberty told me, almost with awe, about his young charges. "They are amazing, extraordinary," he stated. "Even the most gravely wounded only want to return to their comrades. They feel guilty about not being at the front. It does not matter where they come from, whether they are religious or not, what their political views are. There is something very beautiful about it. It may sound chauvinistic, but I say this is the eternal spirit of Israel."

On the way back, in a military traffic jam that stretched for several miles, I met an old radio colleague who was going to see his wounded son, Ayal. A stocky, bespectacled Yemenite, he was not wearing his usual smile. His plump wife stood by his side, trying not to look worried. She wasn't very good at it. "It wasn't too serious; he will be all right," he reassured me. I wished him a speedy recovery for his son and went on my way.

I spoke to Ayal a few months later, in his parents' Jerusalem apartment. He was about to be discharged from the army and was looking forward to going abroad. There was no trace of the burns he had suffered on his face, a face of special Yemenite beauty, lit up occasionally with a dazzling smile. He smoked nervously during our conversation and fondled a young puppy. His recollections were still vivid.

He had wanted to go to war, he confessed. His unit had been rushed to the northern border six or seven times and they were getting tired of the false alarms. He had practiced in his tank for three years and he wanted to test himself, to see whether he could stand up to the real thing.

He thought it was justified to push the PLO out of range of the northern settlements, possibly even to chase them out of Beirut. "We had absolutely no idea of where we were going," he told me. "I thought we would get to the Litani River and then see, but we crossed the Litani and kept on going."

His first test had come just past Sidon, when he heard over the radio that the commander of another tank had been hit. "Deadly fear," was how he described it. It never left him during the following days.

"The combined PLO-Syrian force was running between the tanks and firing rocket-propelled grenades. We were firing back with all we had. I once heard that, in the thick of battle, your fear disappears. It wasn't like that with me."

He very soon lost his thirst for battle. War, he told me, was the most terrible thing that people could do to each other. "One minute you see a live human being and, in a second, he is a mess, plastered over a vehicle. You want God to come down from the sky and put a stop to it."

South of Beirut, his tank was hit by a Sagger missile and caught fire. He felt a hot blow in the face and went over the side. His only thought was flight — he had even abandoned his weapon. He showed me a burned, blackened, twisted piece of metal, part of the remains of his tank. It spoke even louder than his words.

The pain came about a quarter of an hour later, and even morphine injections could not stop it. Only after he had been helicoptered to the hospital did it die down. The sight of his blistered face in the mirror had been a shock, but he was not too badly burned and made his own phone call to tell his parents.

What really worried him about this war, he told me, was the degenerating effect of occupying South Lebanon, a populated area. When he returned to his unit, he found that looting was almost a way of life, even though the front-line units behaved better than the service crews who came afterward.

Outright looting was usually prevented and often punished, he conceded, but he was just as worried about the stealing from offices and buildings of the UN, of which even some officers were guilty. "Mostly it was not personal," he said. "They would take a rug or a filing cabinet for the unit back home. But what difference does it make? Stealing is stealing." The soldiers had spent prodigious efforts on acquiring tape recorders and video systems. Often they bought them legitimately, but then came the "fun" of smuggling them back past the border.

"Next time we go to war," he said in disgust, "the soldiers will be thinking about the videos they want to take home, not about the war."

He was also concerned about the bombing in Beirut, some of which he had witnessed. "You want to believe it is pinpoint bombing," he said, shaking his head, "but when you see the destruction you can't say we didn't kill civilians."

I asked him whether he was still proud to be a soldier in the IDF, and he smiled and admitted, "Not quite as much as before."

Ayal's experience was typical of many young soldiers': confusion coupled with eagerness at first, then doubts, and finally qualified disapproval. The critics of the war tended, for the most part, to be reserve soldiers. The young conscripts were, in my experience, more supportive, but even the most belligerent of them showed some doubt beneath the surface.

I met Michael up near the Lebanese border at Metulla, where he had just returned from a spell of patrol duty. Dark, well-built, with a prominent nose and a particularly heavy growth of stubble, Michael wore the knitted skullcap of the religious youth movement *B'nai Akiva*. His unit was made up mostly of students from an agricultural boarding school south of Haifa.

"It is absurd to think that we could have stopped at forty-five kilometers," he told me belligerently, softening it with a smile.

"Maybe it was a mistake to go to war at all?" I suggested diffidently.

"Now you are talking nonsense." He shook his head sadly. "You do realize that you are talking nonsense, don't you?"

The Palestinians, he informed me, lived by the gun. He wished that he could show me the picture he had found of a kid, who could not have been more than eight years old, toting a Kalashnikof assault rifle. "The Klatch was bigger than him!" He laughed.

He went on to describe the weapons dumps his units had found in the Rashadiya refugee camp. There had been hundreds of crates of shells and rockets and bullets. "They had so many grenades," he said, "do you realize how much damage they could have done?"

There had been no choice but to go to war and, once you started, you had to finish. Yes. Even invade West Beirut. Arafat had to be kicked out. If it could be done without a fight, so much the better, but only because of the casualties on our side. He didn't care about the terrorists.

I asked him about the Lebanese civilians, and he shrugged and noted that they had harbored the terrorists. The IDF had given out leaflets, spoken through loudspeakers, done everything to give the civilians a chance to get away. Too much, in his view — it had endangered the lives of our soldiers. He had no scruples about the bombing, he insisted. It was better than our boys being killed.

I asked him whether he thought the Palestinian problem could be solved by force. "You know what the Phalangists say," was his brutal reply. "Kill them while they are still young!"

One of his comrades smiled and made a motion, opening and shutting his hand, to indicate that Michael was only talking. Michael saw him and laughed. "He is right," he told me. "I talk big, but when it comes to it I am sorry for them." His friends told me that Michael had intervened to prevent another soldier from beating a prisoner and had given the prisoner water.

"Isn't there any right on their side?" I asked. He considered this. Well, he supposed they believed in their cause. Everyone fights for what he believes in. They had some right on their side, he thought. "They want their state as we wanted ours thirty years ago, but we were more constructive. They are the ones who want to fight. If they want a state, let them come and talk to us."

Could they have a state if they came and negotiated? No, he didn't really think so. It would be dangerous to have a state on the West Bank. Let them go to Jordan.

Avner, Michael's commander, was a graduate of a *hesder* yeshiva, a seminary that combines military service with Jewish religious study. Blond, serious, wearing steel-rimmed glasses, knitted skullcap perched on his curls, he justified the war absolutely. The terrorists had hit Kiryat Shmona, Nahariya, and many other places and, if Israel had not struck, they would have done so again. According to the Torah (the first five books of the Old Testament), he explained, it is perfectly justifiable to kill someone who wants to kill you. "It was enough that I heard the babies crying in Misgav Am," he told me. He must have been in the unit that stormed the baby house.

His religious beliefs forbade him to harm civilians, he informed me, but any surgery hurt, and sometimes you had to cut off a limb to keep the body healthy. The most moral thing, in his view, was to bring the soldier back whole to his mother. In this war the army had exaggerated its care for civilians. In the refugee camps the terrorists were firing from behind civilians and the soldiers had not fired back.

His most difficult moment had come when he found the body of his missing company commander in an orchard. The man had apparently been made to dig his own grave before being shot.

"I have seen people blown to bits," he told me, "but this was a rotting corpse, it was decaying." On the one hand, he thought, there is a world where scientists spend years in researching cures for cancer or other diseases. On the other hand, instant destruction. "Not just a body," he mused. "A human soul. That is a big thing for a believer. Life is a miracle. Look at the size of an artificial kidney. Will man ever succeed in manufacturing an eye?"

But the war had not weakened his belief. On the contrary, he had been strengthened. Life was more precious to him now; it had more significance. Yet, he admitted, he was much more tense than he had been. Once he used to dance the hora with the boys at the yeshiva for hours on end. He could not do this anymore, could not unwind. When he went home on leave, he behaved as if he were on patrol. The slightest movement made him jump. He wanted to leave Lebanon and never go back there. But if he had to, he would fight again.

There would always be wars, he informed me. It was the Jewish fate, which he accepted gladly. He would not buy peace by giving up parts of the Holy Land.

The Palestinians? They could be residents, but they had to accept Jewish rule. If they behaved themselves, fine. If not, they could be packed across the border. Judea and Samaria must be settled. They belonged to the Jewish people and there was no compromise possible. If we had to fight for it, so be it.

Avner is a very special case, a supporter of the extreme nationalist-religious line, and Michael, too, is from the religious youth movement, which tends to take a militant stand in Israeli policy toward the Arabs and in particular the Palestinians. But there is little doubt that the young conscript soldiers generally were eager to test themselves in battle and generally also were more supportive of the war than their older fellow soldiers in the reserve.

My son, Etan, at twenty-three, found himself between the two worlds. He was near enough to his conscript service to remember how he felt then, but in the war he found himself serving with older soldiers. While he was a veteran of the Litani operation, most of his fellow warriors had also fought in the Yom Kippur War.

He recalled how, as a conscript, he had lain in ambush for a terrorist gang near the river Jordan. A member of another ambush had opened fire prematurely, with the result that the gang fled and there was no battle. He had felt disappointment.

At the outset of the Lebanon war, he thought straight-away that it was a mistake. Very early on, he told a friend, "It was not even worth it for the first pilot who was shot down." But, once mobilized, he explained, you simply do not have time to think. You have your job, which is to advance and achieve and your mind is just on that. If the civilians are caught up in the momentum of developments, with the soldiers it is even more so.

As time went on, however, he began to think. He noted that the divisional commander was thirsty for action — and possibly glory — but that the company commander was not at all inclined to "look for danger." There were strong doubts about Beirut, he told me, and even stronger ones about the necessity of conflict with the Syrians. As the scale of the conflict became clearer, he wrote to me: "In our unit, I can tell you, the enthusiasm for 'Arik Sharon's war' is as near to zero as you can get!"

The government was quick to blame the media for the doubts about the war. Sharon quoted an anonymous soldier as pointing at a bundle of newspapers and saying, "Here comes the poison." But the first questioning about war aims came from the soldiers themselves.

Ze'ev Schiff, the experienced military correspondent of *Ha'aretz*, wrote that the most lively arguments were among the troops "who are fighting this war and paying for it with their lives." This dispute, he noted, would have taken place regardless of the media or the home front.

The government's information effort, both at home and abroad, was a failure, he asserted. It was also a failure among the troops, "who do not know what they are fighting for." At the outset, wrote Schiff, the doubters were in a minority, but later, in certain front-line units, they became a majority.

The Labor opposition in the Knesset found itself in a tricky position. Taken into Sharon's confidence at the start of the war, and more or less approving the first forty-five kilometers, it was afraid of seeming unpatriotic in time of war. But toward the end of June the opponents of the war started to make themselves heard, particularly among reserve soldiers who had been discharged after their first tour of duty.

An antiwar demonstration in Tel Aviv drew an estimated ten thousand, many of them discharged soldiers, and another group of soldiers organized a loose association, which they called Soldiers against Silence. At a news conference they called for the dismissal of Sharon, scrupulous maintenance of the cease-fire, and a realization that the Palestinian problem could not be solved by force.

They then pitched a tent outside the prime minister's office in Jerusalem and started a protest vigil. It was there, on June 29, in the fourth week of the war, that I spoke to Shuki. Shuki is definitely not someone you would look at twice if you passed him in the street. He is short and slight, with close-cropped sandy hair, freckled face, and gray-green eyes that are slightly bloodshot on this sunny morning, for he and his friends have had a rough night. A mob of pro-government supporters, fresh from a public rally, had fallen on them and ripped their tent to shreds.

A twenty-seven-year-old graduate student of history and philosophy at the Hebrew University, Shuki is married to a psychologist. He shakes his head and laughs ruefully when I ask him if he is a member of a kibbutz. *Kibbutznik*, he explains, was one of the terms of abuse flung at him and his friends by the mob. Another expletive was *Ashkenazi*, which means "Jews of European origin."

Some of Begin's most fervent supporters were to be found among the oriental Jewish community. Although most of them had arrived in Israel after the Europeans were established, they make up the majority of the lower-income groups and tend to resent their fellow citizens from Europe. Many saw in Begin, the former outsider and loser who made it, their champion. His hard-line foreign policy was certainly no handicap in maintaining their support.

Shuki, a veteran of both the Yom Kippur War and the recent conflict, had suffered his first "war wounds" at the hands of these youths.

"Didn't you explain that you had fought in the war?" I asked.

"They didn't want to listen," replied Shuki sadly. "They were full of hatred. It was clear that they had been stirred up." His tone was one of regret rather than anger. There was an aura of gentleness about Shuki, not unusual in members of the elite units of the IDF. An NCO in the paratroop reserve, he had fought at the Chinese Farm on the Suez Canal in the Yom Kippur War, one of the most savage battles in our country's history.

"I knew exactly why I was there," he said, recalling the 1973 war. "I knew who the enemy was and where he was. I knew that we had to fight through to the bridgehead, whatever the danger. I knew that if not for us, the Egyptian army could have broken through toward Tel Aviv. We fought to defend our parents and our children. There was no alternative."

The Lebanon war, in his opinion, was different. It was not a war for Israel's survival. He agreed that the PLO was a savage enemy; he had seen their enormous depots of arms and ammunition. But, as far as he was concerned, the war proved one thing: the Palestinian problem is political and cannot be solved by military means.

Shuki and his comrades had taken the Palestinian refugee camp of En Hilwe after one of the fiercest battles of the recent war. *Camp* is really not the best word to describe the slum neighborhood on the outskirts of Sidon, inhabited almost entirely by Palestinians who fled from Israel in 1948 or from Jordan in 1970. The area was shelled and bombed for almost a week before they went in. Shuki thought that most of the casualties were innocent civilians, because the PLO men were safe in their bunkers. The destruction had made the subsequent battle harder, he thought, as it had been more difficult to move through the ruins than through buildings that were still standing. They fought their way through the neighborhood carefully, even fastidiously, checking each wall, each room, each ruined building. Some members of his unit had been wounded by a grenade thrown from a bunker as they tried to check out a room for noncombatants.

"We were making the moral equation all the time," he maintained. "But those who sent us were not." They had been ordered not to harm women and children, but "when you are ordered to advance, shooting into an inhabited area, such an order is *shtuyot bemitz*" (a childish expression meaning "absolute nonsense"). There had been, he informed me, *tohar haneshek*, literally "purity of arms," but only of light arms — not of heavy weapons. (Tohar haneshek is an old IDF concept inherited from the pre-state Haganah defense force. Often translated as "fighting clean," it involves maintaining humane norms in battle, avoiding civilian casualties and treating prisoners decently.) There was no tohar of bombs and artillery, he noted. How could there have been?

"The bombing was not indiscriminate," he conceded. "But when you drop hundreds of bombs and fire hundreds of rounds of artillery, how can you avoid harming noncombatants?"

He had not been trained for this sort of war, he told me. "I was trained to fight face to face with the enemy, but who was the enemy — what was he, where was he? The children were running about under our feet!"

On one occasion he had been leading his squad down an alley when two old men popped up twenty yards away, begging them not to shoot. They had ceased fire and shouted to the old men to leave the area. Instead, the men had hauled out a crate of Pepsi-Cola for the soldiers. "They simply wanted to give us drinks," exclaimed Shuki. "Two hundred yards away — even a hundred — they would have been targets. We would have fired at them and been glad to hit them. So when does a human being become a target? Is it a question of distance?"

His soldiers had been trained to attack a fortified position, to cross a ditch, to penetrate barbed wire, to disable a tank — not to fight among old men and children. It was an absurd picture. They would fight their way through a bunker and then take a rest. They would sit there, with their guns, ammunition, helmets, and flak jackets, and argue about the war.

"You carry your moral burden with you wherever you go," he noted. "You don't stop being a human being because you are fighting for your life. I have just read about the Falkland Islands war and I am disgusted with the British. Their war was even more unjust, but there does not seem to have been any protest among the soldiers or the people.

"That is the dilemma of the Israeli soldier. We live in a democracy, but we have to obey orders. You go out there and you fight and do a good job, but when you come back you have to do what your conscience tells you."

He knew they had fought well, he said, and that was why it hurt when certain politicians accused them of "sticking a knife in the nation's back." They had made their statement in En Hilwe and now they were making it again in Jerusalem.

Maybe, I suggested, there was no solution without a war. He had fought the Egyptians with a clear conscience, a long way from home. In this war, Israel was fighting the Palestinians for the Land of Israel.

At this point, Doron, a fellow demonstrator, joined in. A burly, red-faced armored corps soldier with black, curly hair, Doron had been wounded in the Yom Kippur War and hospitalized for five months. In Lebanon he had fought against the Syrians on the eastern front.

The implication of my remarks was terrible, he said. If I had told his parents, who had come to Israel in the 1930s, that there would be a war every ten years, it would not have been worthwhile to establish the state. He was not prepared to tell his children that they faced unending warfare. The war with the Palestinians must be finished, just as the war with the Egyptians had been. He agreed with the initial action in this war, with pushing the PLO back out of range. It was what happened subsequently that upset him. But, even now, he would forgive the leadership if they would talk to the Palestinians.

"I would support Begin and Sharon, despite all the lies they told," declared Doron. "If they would talk to the PLO, I would kiss their hands and feet. You can only make peace with your enemies."

Shuki kept nodding his head in agreement during Doron's statement and added, "You know what grated on my ears today in the Knesset? They talked about civilian casualties, but only about *Lebanese* casualties. Aren't the Palestinians human beings?"

They were speaking angrily, cutting in on one another. The leaders had lied. Begin had spoken in the Knesset about forty kilometers or forty-five, but they had never heard these figures all the time they were fighting. Sharon had "led the country by the nose."

At this point I challenged them again. The war was a month old, I noted, and now the terrorists were holed up in Beirut. Whatever the rights or wrongs of the war, surely we all agreed that it would be a good thing to kick the PLO out of the Lebanese capital. Demonstrations like theirs were liable to encourage the

PLO to sit tight. This made an IDF thrust into West Beirut more likely and increased the chances of bloodshed on all sides.

Shuki sighed deeply, and we sat in silence for a few minutes. "I owe you an answer on that," he admitted at length. "I find it difficult to think logically. Here we are, sitting in the shade outside the prime minister's office in Jerusalem, wearing clean clothes, discussing the situation rationally.

"At the same time I am back in the hell of En Hilwe: filthy, dirty, unshaven, loaded down with weapons and ammunition, and wondering where it is all going to end. It is all still with me. Give me a bit more time and maybe I will be able to go into an air-conditioned room and work it all out.

"Right now, I just want to stop the shooting at once. If the political leaders would look into the eyes of the soldiers going to battle, it might teach them something. You have to be an idiot if you think we can go into West Beirut without it costing hundreds of lives — ours and theirs."

That was the reason they were organizing. The movement had started spontaneously in each unit. The first thing was to demand Sharon's resignation. "He postures as the great leader, borne on the shoulders of the troops. Well, he is not being borne by us!"

Did this mean he would refuse to serve? No. He expected to be recalled soon, and he would be proud to go and serve with the paratroops again. He had no regrets about volunteering for this elite unit nine years ago. He was in a company that retained its humanity, and the soldiers did their best not to harm civilians or their property. If he ever found himself in a situation where his comrades behaved barbarously, he would sit in jail with a clear conscience; but this had not happened.

I left Shuki and his friends with a clear perception that we were reaching a watershed. If the government was losing the confidence of the front-line troops, the situation was serious. It was not enough to command a majority in the country. For war the majority had to be decisive and it had to include the Shukis and the Dorons, and the Yigals, Dudus, Amis, Ayals, Ronens, Orans, and all the young sabras (Israeli-born) on whom our lives depended.

Early in July Hirsh Goodman, military correspondent of the *Jerusalem Post*, described a visit to the front lines, in which he and two colleagues were surrounded by officers and men of four top fighting units who accused them of covering up the truth, of lying to the public, of not reporting on the real mood at the front, and of being lackeys of the defense minister. "We were accused by the overwhelming majority of the men — including senior officers — of allowing this war to grow out of all proportion to the original goals," he wrote.

Ezer Weizman wrote disparagingly of the Peace Now movement in his book *The Battle for Peace*, but he added the following sentence about the young members: "These were just the type of young men into whose eyes I wanted to be able to look with a clear conscience, should I ever have to order them to go to war." Weizman knows what he is talking about and he knows how much we rely on the special elite units and their superb young soldiers. These young men, who know better than anyone else what war is all about, are prepared to go and fight only if they are convinced that there is no alternative. That has always been the moral basis for the wars of Israel.

So, even though the public opinion polls showed a thumping 90 percent of Israelis in favor of the war, government supporters would have been well advised to worry about the quality of those in opposition. Furthermore, a private street poll which I conducted in Jerusalem around that time showed me that the situation was more complex than it seemed, even with regard to the general public.

Of the twenty-six people I polled, fully eighteen pronounced themselves in favor of the campaign, but once I got beyond the simple yes/no questions, there was a large amount of confusion. Very few were in favor all along the line, and even those who were said they did not think it would solve anything. Half of those in favor said that it had gone far enough, and opposed pushing into West Beirut.

By contrast, one woman who said she was against the war and would come and help me "hang Sharon in person" abused me for asking questions. It was treasonable of me, she opined, to walk about questioning people. "My son is at the front," she declared, "and we must not do anything to demoralize the boys there."

This is a factor that should not be underestimated in assessing the support for the war shown in the polls. In a country like Israel, small and surrounded by enemies, there is a strong reluctance to "rock the boat." Even those doubtful about the war hesitated before speaking out, which makes the fact of opposition, while the guns were still firing, even more remarkable.

On Saturday, July 3, an antiwar demonstration organized by the Peace Now movement was reportedly attended by one hundred thousand people. I was not among them; my own feelings were still ambivalent. My sympathies were with Shuki, Doron, and the other protesters, but I also felt, paradoxically, that there was now a better than even chance of making a deal with the Palestinians. "Maybe it takes a Begin and a Sharon to deal with a Yasir Arafat," I wrote to a friend. The irony was that the very men who had created the situation were the least capable of taking advantage of it.

There were the Palestinians, besieged in Beirut, abandoned by their Arab allies, their Soviet allies, and their Third World allies. Now was the time to step forward and say, "We are the only friends you have. Come on, let's negotiate and divide up what we call Israel and you call Palestine between us." But Begin, with his firm belief that the land of Israel — all of it — belongs eternally to the Jews, and Sharon, with his belief that strength is the answer to everything, would be the last people to do this.

My own visits to Lebanon during the first weeks of the war did little to resolve my ambivalence, for I found it difficult to disapprove entirely of our presence there. On one trip I counted twenty trucks and light pickups traveling south, loaded with mattresses, furniture, and kitchen equipment. The Lebanese were returning to their homes, which had been liberated from the PLO. There was plenty of evidence — at least during those first weeks — that the local population was pleased to be occupied by the IDF.

I had served in Gaza in 1970, at the height of terrorist activity, and I know what a frightened, occupied population looks like. There, the young women had ignored us, hurrying hastily by. The young men had stared resentfully and then averted their gaze as we approached. The children had hurled abuse — and stones — at our patrols; they fled out of harm's way when we got too near.

It wasn't like that in Lebanon. The people were friendly and curious, approaching both soldiers and visitors with questions. Smiles were far more frequent than scowls, and for the most part, people went about their business with manifest unconcern.

Driving across the border at Rosh Hanikra aroused an unreal feeling, rather like walking into East Jerusalem in 1967. Israel is a claustrophobic country, although less than it was. We can now go to Egypt, but Jordan, Syria, and (until recently) Lebanon were still non-countries. They flickered on our television screens, but we could not drive along their roads, walk their streets, or climb their hills. Crossing the border, I almost expected to fall off the end of the world. And then the real paradox: the country was very much like ours. It had the same rocks, the same sea, the same vegetation.

The roads were inferior, but the cultivation was even more intensive. Every little patch of land was used for growing citrus fruit, bananas, or corn. The citrus orchards were bordered with gray cinder-block walls, unlike those in Israel. Two men in *keffiye* headdresses were working on an ancient threshing machine, and I felt a desire to bring them the modernity of Israeli agriculture: combine harvesters, drip irrigation, new methods of fertilization. I thought of my son, a student of agricultural engineering at the

Haifa Technion, now a soldier in the army of occupation. Would he one day return to Lebanon as an "expert" to make amends for the destruction?

We stopped briefly in Tyre and Sidon — only long enough to see that the towns had not been destroyed, as reported in the international media. But the contention of Ya'acov Meridor, an Israeli cabinet minister, that "only ten houses in Tyre" had been destroyed was patently ludicrous.

Blackened, damaged buildings lurched drunkenly. Shop fronts were empty and deserted, most of them without glass. Some buildings, although still standing, were no more than shells; others had enormous cracks down their sides. Most of the buildings had not been seriously damaged, but many were pockmarked with bullet holes and some had gaping holes from shellfire. Craters of varying sizes disfigured the streets and squares. The rubble was everywhere and the broken glass crunched under our feet. A mosque, clearly untouched, loomed among the damaged buildings. The smell of burning still lingered.

Some of the damage was clearly pre-invasion. Together with a journalistic colleague, I counted sixty damaged buildings in one neighborhood, and we agreed that about two-thirds had been hit recently. It was an impression, not a statistic.

Outside the town we saw women and children from a nearby Palestinian camp; they were living in the citrus groves under transparent plastic sheeting. An IDF water tanker was dispensing water, and the queue for it was over a hundred yards long. Farther along the road, the gas queue was much longer, stretching for almost a mile.

North of Damur we were stopped by a roadblock. A group of five prisoners sat in the shade of a bridge, heads shaved, hands tied behind their backs. They looked all of fourteen years old. The IDF soldiers who were guarding them told us that they had been turned in by the local villagers, who had accused them of stealing.

After a slight delay we received permission to go on to Beirut.

Begin had announced the same day that the IDF had no intention of entering Beirut. I presumed he meant West Beirut, because the IDF was already right in the heart of the eastern part of the capital.

Black-bereted Phalangist militiamen waved us past roadblocks. Their uniforms, smartly turned out, distinguished them from the crumpled, hatless, unshaven Israeli soldiers. They all wore olive-green, American-style uniforms.

In Beirut there was chaos: the traffic was being directed by IDF soldiers, Lebanese soldiers, Phalangist militiamen, Lebanese police, Lebanese military police, and at least three other forces, which we were unable to identify. There was double-parking, triple-parking, driving on the left, right, and in the center. Everyone was cheerful and friendly and I saw no accidents.

I wore my white sunhat with the legend "Welcome to Israel" emblazoned on it in blue. "Welcome to Beirut," countered several passers-by, pointing at it.

"George," wearing a grimy white shirt and dark blue suit-pants, shakes his brick-red, wrinkled face. "The Syrians are thieves and tramps," he declares loudly. "The Palestinians are worse!" Is he telling us what he thinks we want to hear? "I am not afraid of anyone," he continues. "I don't mind you Israelis coming here. I would like to visit Jerusalem."

He points to a sandbagged shop front. "Look at that: that is against bombs and shells. That is because of the Palestinians."

"Can there be peace now?"

"Why not?" he demands. "In the past we got on well with the Muslims and even with the Jews. I don't say we can have peace with the extremists who just shout, '*Allahu Akbar*' [God is great] and want to kill us, but we can with most Muslims."

"What about the Israelis?"

"Well, they are our friends now. They are helping us. How do you say it? We must cooperate with the devil."

"The Israelis are the devil?"

"No, I didn't mean that." He laughs loudly. "They are welcome. We will start to build our country again. It is a beautiful country."

He gesticulates angrily at the ruined buildings, the rubble and sandbags. "Beirut is as beautiful as Tel Aviv and Haifa," he says.

Far more beautiful, I thought, as I regarded the panorama of the Lebanese capital spread beneath me. It was half an hour later and I was standing in the hills to the east. Across the valley, not two hundred yards away, was the official residence of the Lebanese president, a building of sand-colored cubes surrounded by neatly trimmed box hedges. It was cool up in the hills under the shade of the pine trees. The wooded suburbs of Beirut, with their elegant villas and attractive red-tiled churches, led down to the city below, where modern apartment blocks and hotels were interspersed with parks and open areas. Beyond them the clear blue Mediterranean sparkled in the afternoon sun. It was difficult to believe that we were looking at a battlefield.

"I feel quite at home here already," said Uri, a young paratroop officer. "It is a bit like all three major towns in Israel. The hills are farther from the sea than Haifa, so the downtown part is flat and rather like Tel Aviv. Up here, of course, it's like the Carmel part of Haifa, but if you go a mile or so to the east, the land becomes more bare and it's quite like Jerusalem."

Uri told us that his unit had been welcomed in the Christian villages with rice and flowers, fruit and cold drinks. "We really did feel we were liberating them," he insisted.

Two pretty girls, wearing slacks and sleeveless blouses, came over to talk to us. They were studying at the college beside which Uri and his unit were stationed.

"Are you pleased the Israelis came?" asked one of the soldiers. They shrugged and smiled.

One of the girls, Gracia, said, "We don't want anyone — not the Syrians or the Palestinians — only the Lebanese army."

"We were pleased when the Syrians came at first," added her companion, Claude, "but now we want everyone to go and leave us in peace." She pointed at the presidential palace. "That should be the government again."

On the way back we stopped briefly at Damur to see a church that had been used as a base by the PLO. The benches and the altar had been removed. The floor was covered with rubble and excrement. There were bullet holes everywhere, including the crucifix and the stained-glass windows.

"You see?" demanded our IDF guide. "See what the PLO did?" It would have been more effective if he had kept silent.

On a later visit to Lebanon, in mid-July, the coastal road was far more lively, with the traffic on the narrow highway sometimes six abreast. In contrast to my earlier visits, the cafés and shops were full and doing brisk business. The fruit and vegetable markets were overflowing with oranges, grapefruits, tomatoes, corn, and watermelon. Trucks, piled with household goods, continued to move south.

In Sidon I sat down at a sidewalk café and ordered coffee. The cardamom-flavored coffee was sweet and strong. It came with a glass of cold water and, together with a rather soapy-tasting pistachio cake, cost about a dollar. I paid in Israeli currency.

I noticed IDF soldiers walking around the shops singly. This would never have been permitted in Gaza, where soldiers were always ordered to move in groups of at least three. The streets were still full of rubble, but some cleaning operations were going on. Rebuilding was proceeding apace. In the shell of a bank building, a clerk sat at his desk, exposed to the outside, and attended to customers.

The IDF siege of West Beirut was in full swing and, back at our lookout post above the city, near the presidential palace, we were briefed by an IDF colonel.

"We don't intend to let Habib mess about for a year." He was referring to the ongoing negotiations being conducted by Philip Habib to effect a withdrawal of PLO and Syrian forces from the Lebanese capital. "It is not really a siege. We keep them guessing. The one thing that we want to avoid is the establishment of a new status quo. We are keeping the situation fluid. So one day we

let people in and the following day we don't. One day we shut
down the water; the next night it is the turn of the electricity.
Sometimes we let in food supplies and sometimes we don't."

He was evasive about cooperation with the Phalangists. He
would not even describe it as "cooperation," calling it rather "an
identity of interests." The aim of both parties was to get the PLO
out of Beirut without a fight. Sometimes there was shooting.
Often the IDF didn't even bother to fire back. As if to illustrate
his words, there was a burst of gunfire below, its clattering boom
echoing across the city.

The cutting off of food and water — albeit intermittently — to the
civilian population of West Beirut provoked anger and shame in
Israel. The occasional bombing and shelling provoked even more:
there was a growing feeling that we were behaving as we had
not behaved in the past.

And yet there was still an ambivalence. The dilemma of liberal-
minded Israelis was eloquently expressed in the *Jerusalem Post*
by its diplomatic correspondent, David Landau: "Can we suffer
the jeering, smirking face of Yasir Arafat on our television each
night or bear to see him feted in foreign capitals, still vowing the
eventual establishment of a secular democratic Palestine in place
of Jewish Israel?" Leaving the PLO in Beirut, he argued, would
mean an end to hope of a constructive dialogue between Israelis
and Palestinians. "With the PLO victorious in Beirut, that longed-
for evolution of Israeli public opinion — the de-demonization of
the Palestinians — would sink ever deeper beneath the layers of
misconception and demagoguery." He concluded: "Today we are
at the gates of Beirut. 'We' means Sharon and Raful [the IDF
chief of staff] and Likud and Labor and you and I. For in the war
against the PLO, however wrongheaded and misguided this campaign is, there are no distinctions — because a PLO victory will
be a victory over all of us, not just over Ariel Sharon." The wording
of Landau's article illustrates vividly the extent to which the war
had become personalized and identified with the minister of
defense.

Medad Allon, a soldier serving in Lebanon, wrote a letter to the press in the early days of the war, but he was killed before he could send it. His friends found it and sent it for him, but first they read it to his unit:

"We are the generation of Arik Sharon. We have paid and are paying the tax daily. Parts of bodies, burnt limbs, people loaded with complexes are being brought to Sharon's giant altar. Sharon, you move flags, you play with soldiers, you, it seems, enjoy all this. But I die from this.

"You can say that the nation is behind you, but only a few return home with bloodstains on their clothing, still stunned and silent, tired of wars."

Medad Allon spoke directly to Sharon; my son was only one of the many who agreed when he wrote in his letter home about "Arik Sharon's war." Sharon did not merely symbolize the war, he dominated it. His high-pitched, lisping voice blanketed the airwaves. His words were blazoned across our headlines; his huge, looming, threatening figure filled our television screens.

"Well, at least he scares the Arabs," remarked a journalist colleague who supported the war.

"Scares the *Arabs*," I retorted. "What do you think he does to *me*?"

Never at a loss for words, always on the move, whether riding, helmeted, in a jeep through Beirut or trading brickbats in the Knesset, he rarely left our consciousness.

"I suggest that all of us show a little more stamina," he kept repeating. He had stamina. Stamina, indeed, is the secret of Sharon's success — if *success* is the right word.

Even before the Lebanon war, Ariel Sharon had been a controversial figure. In his biography of Israel's first prime minister, Michael Bar-Zohar quotes Ben-Gurion as saying, "If Sharon would overcome his defects of not speaking the truth and indulging in gossip, he would be an exemplary military leader."

Begin was always one of Sharon's most fervent admirers, yet in a 1980 newspaper interview he remarked, "Sharon might sur-

round the prime minister's office with tanks." Later he tried to
pass this off as a joke, but in his book, Ezer Weizman wrote that
the prime minister's protestations were hollow, and asserted that
"Begin really believes that Sharon is capable of doing such a
thing."

Born on a moshav in 1928, Sharon first gained prominence as
the commander of Unit 101, a paramilitary group formed to counter
Arab infiltration into Israel in the early 1950s. In 1949, after the
War of Independence, Egypt, Syria, Jordan, and Lebanon signed
armistice agreements with Israel, but they did not accept the
Jewish state. They encouraged infiltration across the borders and
promoted a campaign of murder and sabotage. It was not a question of the occupied territories then, for the West Bank was part
of Jordan and Gaza was under Egyptian rule. All of Israel was
regarded as "occupied territory."

Unit 101 functioned for less than a year before being incorporated into the new paratroop battalion, and in that time it carried out a number of reprisal raids of unprecedented ruthlessness.
The principle of tohar haneshek was pretty well jettisoned by
Unit 101, under Sharon's command.

In reprisal for the murder of a mother and her two children in
an Israeli border settlement, Unit 101 struck at the village of
Kibiya on the West Bank. Several houses were blown up and the
civilian death toll was sixty-nine. Sharon, who personally com-
manded the operation, claimed afterward that since he had evacuated the civilians from the houses about to be blown up, some
people must have been hiding in cellars.

There were raids of almost equal savagery into Jordanian- and
Egyptian-controlled territory, but the most shocking instance of
Sharon's behavior was his support for a private act of vengeance
in 1955.

Unit 101 included a number of officers and soldiers who later
became prominent IDF commanders, but its most famous combat
soldier was a young man named Meir Har-Zion. He was an ad-
venturous type and, while still in his teens, had made trips across

the border with his sister, Shoshana. On one of these trips, the youngsters had been held prisoner by the Syrians for several months.

With her brother mobilized into the IDF, Shoshana and another girl set out for the Jordanian city of Petra, where their adventure ended in tragedy. They were discovered and murdered by a Bedouin tribe in the Judean desert north of En Gedi by the Dead Sea.

Taking three comrades with him, Har-Zion crossed the border and murdered five members of the Bedouin tribe, which he held responsible for the death of his sister and her friend.

Sharon, by now commander of the paratroop battalion, had supplied the four with transport, weapons, food, and other equipment. Only the intervention of Ben-Gurion himself (who, despite his reservations about Sharon's character, admired his daring and ingenuity) prevented Sharon's dismissal from the army. In the besieged Israel of the 1950s, BG apparently felt that a fighting spirit should be fostered. It is a shame he forgot, temporarily, his obsession about Israel's being a "light unto the nations," but then he probably never guessed that, one day, the daring major would be defense minister of the State of Israel.

In 1968 Meir Har-Zion published a diary of his army exploits, for which Sharon wrote the introduction. The problem of Arab terrorism, he wrote, would not be solved, even by peace with the Arab states. It was a war to the death: either the terrorists would destroy Israel, or Israel would strike at them and destroy their ability to carry out terrorist raids. The reprisal raids of the 1950s, Sharon indicated, were the correct way. Two decades later, when he became minister of defense, Sharon had not changed his views.

In the 1956 Sinai Campaign, Sharon's unit was parachuted behind enemy lines in Sinai two days before the general attack. He was expressly ordered not to engage the enemy in battle, but he obtained permission for a "reconnaissance patrol" and sent his forces straight into an Egyptian ambush. In the ensuing battle thirty-eight soldiers were killed and one hundred twenty wounded; far from contributing to the success of the campaign, it actually damaged it.

In a newspaper interview, Mordechai Gur, a previous chief of staff who is now a Labor Knesset member, spoke of this incident, in which he had been involved. Sharon, he maintained, had been influenced by the desire to enlarge his own part in the campaign and to improve his personal status. These ambitions, asserted Gur, were already dominant in 1956 and led a number of officers to go to Sharon after the Mitla Pass ambush and tell him that he ought to leave the paratroops. Sharon's essential fault, in Gur's assessment, was a blind belief in force as the solution to problems. Even today, said Gur, he thought as a battalion commander, rather than as a political leader.

In his biography of the late Moshe Dayan, Sharon's superior officer for many years, Shabtai Tevet wrote that in the 1950s Dayan wanted to remove the overly defensive spirit in the IDF after the 1948 war. He wanted his officers to take their objectives "by frontal attack, paying for it with lives," and to exorcise "Jewish cleverness from the IDF." Apparently Sharon learned the lesson well.

As a brigade commander in the Six Day War, Sharon broke through at the key junction of Abu Agheila in Sinai. It was a complicated operation, which won praise from some observers, but veteran military commentator Edgar O'Ballance felt that while it was conducted "with skill and determination," Sharon's plan left his unit battered and weary, "with much of its potential mobility gone."

In the Yom Kippur War of 1973, Sharon, a member of the reserve, led the first Israeli counterattack across the Suez Canal. In view of the fact that Israel had received a severe shock at the hands of the Egyptians and the Syrians, the relief felt at an IDF counterstrike was considerable, and Sharon was hailed as the hero of the war in the media, a status he utilized for a personal conflict against his commanding officers. He spoke out publicly

against the country's leadership, gave battlefield news confer-
ences and interviews in defiance of military regulations, dis-
obeyed orders, and announced to all and sundry that he was
disobeying orders.

Ezer Weizman wrote: "He may be the greatest combat commander of our times, but political life has different values. Sharon
has lost sight of the distinction between his own personal good
and the good of the state."

Shortly before the Yom Kippur War, I heard Sharon's opinion
of Weizman, when I interviewed him for the radio: "Ezer is brilliant," he told me. "But he does not have my stamina. You don't
know me: I can wait twenty years to gain my objective."

A few months before the 1973 war, Sharon had left the army,
after being passed over for the post of chief of staff, and entered
political life. He joined the Liberal party, then part of an alliance
with Begin's Herut.

For years the political right in Israel had been trying to unify
in a political bloc to counter the Labor movement, which had
ruled Israel for twenty-five years. Personalities and factionalism
had prevented this, but within weeks of his entry into politics
Sharon pulled it off and established the Likud bloc, which, although it did not immediately beat Labor, today rules Israel.

I traveled to Sharon's home in Beersheba to ask him how he
had achieved his victory.

"Do I call you Mr. Sharon, or General Sharon?" I opened.

"I'd like you to call me Arik Sharon," he replied with a disarm-
ing smile. He was a comfortable man, stout and good-humored,
with thick, almost white hair and the craggy face of a Roman
senator. We sat in his comfortable lounge, which was furnished
with Persian rugs, ceremonial swords, pistols, and other memora-
bilia. It was difficult to think of this relaxed, smiling man as
formidable. Only his slightly prominent eyes hinted at a thyroid
condition, which might explain his hyperactive personality.

He disposed of my questions with swift assurance, speaking

into the microphone a few well-chosen platitudes that he judged would satisfy the English-speaking radio listeners, and taking care to pay a particularly fulsome tribute to the "statesmanship" of Menachem Begin. He then broke off our conversation to phone Begin for a chat. "I phone him every day," he said shrewdly, "just to keep in touch." He wanted to show that the popular general who had created the Likud bloc was not about to seize the leadership for himself — at least not yet.

Then, while his attractive wife, Lily, served us coffee and cakes and with the tape recorder safely out of the way, he turned to me with a wolfish grin and said, "You asked how I did it; now I'll tell you!"

The details need not occupy us, but I was fascinated by his account of persuasion, charm, flattery, bullying, threats, and ultimatums. I was more impressed by his sheer energy and stamina than by his tactical flair. It was clear to me that he had simply worn out everybody else. He told me he was prepared to wait twenty years, if necessary, to achieve his ends, but he clearly did not think that would be necessary.

He then launched into a two-pronged explanation of his political views, one of which was to be borne out by subsequent events and the other of which was not. Israel, he told me, was a superpower, albeit a small one. The IDF, one of the strongest armies in the world, was fully capable of imposing its will on the neighboring countries. He has remained faithful to this thesis.

His second point concerned his liberalism on domestic matters. The Israeli Arabs, he told me, were getting a very raw deal. "I had in my command Bedouin who penetrated into Egypt and Jordan on intelligence missions and who are not allowed into certain areas of Israel. If I join the government, this discrimination will stop."

When he did finally join the government, four years later, he was responsible, as minister of agriculture, for unprecedented harassment of those same Bedouin. He ordered the destruction of their camps and their expulsion from areas of the Negev desert, where they had lived for years.

But this was only a sideline. His main task as minister was to promote large-scale Jewish settlement in the West Bank. In 1974, after leaving the army again at the end of the Yom Kippur War, he had supported the movement of religious nationalists who were trying to establish settlements in the West Bank in defiance of the decisions of the Labor government. On more than one occasion he told soldiers who had been sent to remove the illegal settlers not to obey orders.

As agriculture minister, he bulldozed his settlement policy through the government in a manner that presaged his technique in the Lebanon war. In an interview in the afternoon paper, *Yediot Ahronot*, Benny Kelter, Sharon's former assistant for settlement matters, told how Sharon had succeeded in by-passing the cabinet with his special Ministerial Committee for Settlement Affairs. The committee, said Kelter, would make decisions that the rest of the cabinet did not know about, and these became operative before the other ministers woke up to challenge them. He used to bring to cabinet meetings small-scale maps, which he showed to ministers from a distance of fifteen yards or more.

Sharon had instructed Kelter in the technique of showing the maps to ministers, pointing out the proposed settlements and then swiftly rolling up the maps again before the ministers could see what he envisaged. According to former chief of staff Gur, Sharon used the same trick in the Lebanon war. "Sharon showed us the map and said the IDF would get as far as the road north of Sidon, but he was pointing farther north," said Gur. "I know Sharon, so I asked him whether the army would get to where he was pointing, or where he said it would reach. He laughed and said only as far as he said; in fact, the IDF had already reached the spot to which he was *pointing*."

Kelter recalled that key ministers — those who might have opposed his settlement plans — did not turn up at meetings of the ministerial committee, and those who came approved the proposals without really knowing what they were about. Sharon often ordered the start of work on settlements before he presented his plans to the committee for their approval.

Kelter's account seems almost incredible, but it is fully consistent with that in Ezer Weizman's book. There was never an overall discussion about West Bank settlement in the cabinet, wrote Weizman. "I was often astounded to find the cabinet being called on to give its retroactive stamp of approval to faits accomplis . . . they automatically bowed to Sharon's views whenever he uttered the word *security*."

As the Lebanon war continued, the criticism in the country grew, both among the various protest groups and, finally, in the Labor party. But Sharon preserved his dominance in the cabinet and continued to impose his will on the nation.

Toward the end of July, Sharon apparently concluded that the efforts of Philip Habib to get the PLO out of Beirut without a fight were not going to be successful. He ordered new call-ups and began to plan actively for the conquest of West Beirut.

There was one place, however, where his maneuvers were treated with ever-increasing suspicion: the IDF, and not just among the junior officers, NCOs, and soldiers of the protest movements. The opposition to the invasion of West Beirut reached the very highest ranks of the army. While most senior officers were satisfied with expressing their views through normal channels, one young officer found this route insufficient.

At first we did not know his name — only that a brigade commander had asked to be relieved of his duties. A few days later his name became public: Colonel Eli Geva, commander of one of the IDF's crack armored brigades. The son of a retired IDF general, Geva, a nonpolitical professional soldier, had been one of the most promising officers in the entire army. He had particularly distinguished himself in the Lebanon war, and his brigade had been one of the first IDF units to reach Beirut.

Sharon and the chief of staff failed to persuade the thirty-two-year-old officer to change his mind, so he was brought before the prime minister himself. This exchange was reported in the press:

Geva: When I look through my binoculars at West Beirut, I can
see young children playing.
Begin: Have you been ordered to fire on children?
Geva: No.
Begin: Then what are you complaining about?

When I spoke to Eli Geva, one year later, he told me that
he had been trying to sharpen the image for the prime
minister; he said the dialogue between them was unimportant.
His question to Begin still stood: What about the fate of those
children, if the IDF had moved in? At the same time, said Geva,
his main consideration had been for the lives of his own
soldiers.

The debate raged throughout the country: in forward positions
in Lebanon and in army camps at home; in private homes and
in the street; on television and in the press. Some of his soldiers
said on television that he had deserted them; others took an
opposing view. "He was acting for those of us who could not do
anything about it," said one. "I think he was one hundred percent
right."

The first thing that struck me when I met Geva was his extreme
youthfulness. He was blue-chinned and rather stout, his unlined
face belying the heavy responsibility that had been laid on his
shoulders. He had been appointed a full colonel at the age of
twenty-seven and had served in the Yom Kippur War as a company commander at the age of twenty-three.

I spoke to him in his modest but comfortable apartment in
Tel Aviv's Ra'ananna suburb. Leora, his wife, slim, attractive,
russet-haired, was cleaning the apartment and putting the children to bed after spending the day studying law at Tel Aviv
University. The television news was screening a report of a
new build-up of tension between Israel and Syria, and Geva admitted a trifle ruefully that he felt rather out of things. Normally
he would have been planning, discussing, organizing the IDF
forces; instead he was commuting daily to his factory manager's

office in the Haifa area. "At times like these you feel you could have made a contribution," he conceded, "but I don't have any regrets."

There was an unwritten contract between a commander and his soldiers, he told me, which said that the commander must do all in his power to safeguard the soldiers' lives and prevent unnecessary casualties. He was concerned about civilian casualties, "but the first consideration was the lives of my own soldiers." The price paid for entering West Beirut, while the PLO and the Syrians were still there, was not worth any gain that might have been achieved.

"Let's say, for the sake of argument, that we had managed to kill and capture half of the PLO men holed up in West Beirut. Would it have solved the problem of terrorism? Would it have solved the Palestinian problem? If force is the only answer, the IDF should not have stopped there. It should have gone on to Tripoli, Damascus, and Amman, the capital of Jordan."

One had to understand the limits of power, declared Geva, and that was precisely what the present leadership had not understood. Strength alone was never a solution; there were other factors as well. Strength had to be used with caution and sophistication.

Geva was not opposed to the use of force as such. He thought the initial drive into Lebanon had been justified. "But we should have concentrated on hitting at those terrorists who posed an immediate threat to our northern settlements. Any idea of imposing a new order on Lebanon, or of destroying the PLO once and for all, was a dangerous illusion."

Had he seen his job, as a professional soldier, as preventing war, I asked him, or had he wanted to put his expertise to the test?

"I'll tell you a story," he said, smiling. "My generation did not fight in the Six Day War or the subsequent War of Attrition on the Suez Canal and the Jordan River. I remember sitting in an army camp with my friend, Rosenzweig, and wondering when we were going to get a chance to fight.

"I met Rosenzweig during a lull in the battle on the Golan Heights in 1973. We were both company commanders in that tough battle and, while our tanks were being armed, we sat and told each other what fools we had been. Two hours later Rosenzweig was killed." He shook his head sadly. "Anyone who has fought in a war doesn't go looking for another one. If you have to fight, you do, but you don't go looking for it."

Geva does not think it wise to try to throw the Palestinians out of South Lebanon. He believes it is in Israel's interest to work with the Lebanese to ensure their integration there. He sees the linkage with the West Bank and feels the Lebanon war came too early for Israel, which had not yet really worked out what it wanted to do about the Palestinian problem. The Lebanon war had forced the Palestinian problem out into the open before the government was really ready for it.

"I am not one of those who disregards our national rights," he said. "But I am not blind to the justice of the other side. The refugees left Israel in 1948. I don't think we can have them back, but we should not forget what happened."

How was it, I asked Geva, that the IDF could have produced two such entirely different officers as Sharon and Geva? He laughed and said there were all sorts in the army.

"Don't get me wrong," he cautioned. "In battle I am for hitting the enemy with all we've got, but I never forget that he is a human being, and that one day I might want to reach an agreement with him."

The fact that the Eli Geva affair was only the tip of an iceberg was acknowledged by Sharon himself, when he said in a television interview that he had been forced to reconsider the mobilization of an elite IDF brigade because of the "national demoralization," which he blamed on the media. A year later he was to blame his own cabinet colleagues, who, he said, started the campaign of demoralization, but that was after subsequent developments. To make his point more dramatic, Sharon claimed that he had not, in fact, mobilized the brigade.

The commander of the brigade in question was understandably

annoyed. Not only had his brigade been mobilized, it was poised to spearhead the invasion of West Beirut. He demanded a public apology from the defense minister. He was quoted in the press as saying, "If the non-call-up of our brigade was the only lie told by Sharon, we might have ignored it. But it comes after a whole string of lies and half-truths. The lack of confidence is there — the army [and the chief of staff] knows it."

So despite the election of Bashir Jemayel as president of Lebanon and the evacuation of the PLO from Beirut at the end of August, the country — and in particular the army — was divided as never before.

Late in August I went to visit my friend Ya'acov at his Jezreel Valley kibbutz, which had been founded by his father's generation fifty years earlier. The founders overcame attacks by local Arabs, poverty, and disease to create a solid, prosperous, communal village deeply rooted in the soil of the land.

Ya'acov personifies the second-generation kibbutznik: tall, broad-shouldered, a natural farmer who has a doctorate in animal genetics. He is the quintessential Israeli — proud, patriotic, a deputy battalion commander in the reserve.

Now he was deeply alienated from his own country. "We do not deserve this disgrace," he protested. "The Jewish people is too great a people to deserve such infamy. We have fought before to defend ourselves, or to achieve our state; but to attack without being attacked first, to bomb civilian areas, to enter an Arab capital — this is shameful! It is the first time we have ever gone to war without a good reason."

So how did it happen? I am back in my room, with my still-sympathetic listeners — at least I hope they are still sympathetic after what I have told them — and they are asking me how Israel acquired Menachem Begin as its prime minister and Ariel Sharon as its defense minister. How did it happen that only four years after it signed a peace treaty with Egypt, the largest of its neighbors, Israel sent its army, artillery, infantry, and air force down the bloody road to Beirut?

2
The Road to Beirut

The Lebanon war was both a deviation from and a culmination of what had gone before. Sharon's former adviser on settlement, Benny Kelter, declared, "The difference between the Labor governments and the Likud is the difference between humanistic Zionism and nationalistic Zionism. When the Jordanians shelled Bet Shean, Moshe Dayan phoned Golda Meir and asked for permission to fire four shells at the Jordanian city of Irbid. Arik Sharon received permission to drop as many bombs as he wanted on Beirut."

Kelter's example is significant, for the Israel Defense Forces fired many more than four shells across the Jordan when Golda Meir was prime minister and Moshe Dayan was defense minister. During the War of Attrition on the Suez Canal, the IDF caused serious destruction to the towns along the waterway.

Dayan was no Sharon, and David Ben-Gurion and Golda Meir were cast in a different mold from Menachem Begin, but Israel was not a pacifist state before Begin came to power. Labor Israel, "the Israel we have seen," was pugnacious in defending itself. Begin was rejected by the Israeli electorate nine times, but Sharon rose through the ranks of the IDF with the support of Ben-Gurion and Dayan. Sharon is far from being a typical IDF officer, but the army always included officers like him, as well as officers like Eli Geva. The difference is that whereas in the past Sharon was the rebel, under Begin it was Geva who became the rebel.

If I were to sum it up in one sentence, I would say that the first forty-five kilometers represented the traditional way of Labor Israel. The expansion of the war was the contribution of Begin and Sharon. I would add that quantity docs affect quality and that I accept Kelter's distinction between humanistic and nationalistic Zionism.

Toward the end of the first month of the war in Lebanon, after the battle for control of the Beirut-Damascus road had cost many lives, Ze'ev Schiff published an article, in *Ha'aretz*, entitled "What are they being killed for?" Schiff quoted Ben-Gurion as saying, "Every Israeli mother should know that her son is in the hands of reliable commanders. They may indeed be compelled to send him to his death, but only if it is vital for the survival of the state." Schiff declared that the battle for the Beirut-Damascus road was definitely not vital for Israel's existence and implied that BG would never have sacrificed young lives for such an objective.

But Ben-Gurion's definition of national survival was, in fact, fairly elastic. In the 1950s, when infiltration and murder were frequent, he approved the establishment of Sharon's Unit 101 and its retaliatory raids across the border. He also personally shielded Sharon and Meir Har-Zion after the latter's act of vengeance for the death of his sister.

Har-Zion published a diary of his early adventures and military operations in which he emerges as daring and courageous, but also utterly ruthless. One can also discern his becoming increasingly cold-blooded as time goes on.

In an early raid across the Sinai border, Unit 101 destroyed a Bedouin camp but did not open fire. "Is this the enemy?" he asks himself. "Is this justifiable? I have not yet felt in my own body the spirit of battle, the thirst for victory, the hatred for the person who wants to take away that which is dearest to you — your life. Those first victories were too easy."

On a later raid there is an armed clash. "The shock and confusion among them is great. Full of satisfaction we drive down the wadi. Only now could we feel the great joy, the joy of victory."

In reprisal for the killing of Israeli soldiers at Bet Guvrin, west of Jerusalem, Har-Zion led a four-man squad to the suburbs of Hebron, where they killed four people. "An Arab is running ahead of us, I bring him down with a burst." A little later: "The operation is over . . . joy bursts over us. We succeeded. A feeling of victory and strength overwhelms us. We are strong. Nothing worries us now . . . Arik [Sharon] meets us with a wide smile and shakes our hands with emotion."

Har-Zion does not describe his vengeance for the death of his sister, but he does write a poem:

I will not cry for you, sister.
Who better than you knows how beautiful was your path,
A free woman, strong, you believed and went forth,
To love your country.
I will not cry for you . . .

If Har-Zion would not cry, other IDF soldiers were not afraid to feel compassion. Both the War of Independence and the Six Day War, even though they were struggles for survival, produced a literature of protest.

Yizhar Smilansky, one of Israel's finest writers, wrote "Khirbet Hizza," a short story about the expulsion of Arab villagers in 1948, which was subsequently televised. In it he depicts the argument between young soldiers who felt revulsion at what they were doing and others who justified their actions. There were more works by Smilansky and others on similar themes.

After the Six Day War, protest was not confined to writers. *The Seventh Day* is an account of a series of conversations with soldiers who fought in that war. A remarkably large number of the soldiers in the elite army units come from the kibbutzim and several writers and editors decided to record the reactions of members of this group, who were brought up to value peace and cooperation.

48   ISRAEL AFTER BEGIN

Intended as an internal kibbutz publication, it became an instant best seller in Israel and was translated into several languages. For the most part, these young kibbutzniks proved to be unlike Har-Zion, who would not cry for his sister. Indeed, one cynical senior IDF officer summed up the book: "They kill and cry and then kill some more and cry some more." For me, the picture that emerges from *The Seventh Day* evokes a source of deep pride in our younger generation; who come across as sensitive, compassionate, and able to put themselves in the position of their enemies.

"I returned without joy. The victory did not mean anything to me ... I never want to go back," an unnamed paratrooper who fought in the Old City of Jerusalem said. "I'll tell you in two words what the battle was: murder and fear. I've had enough.

"We had to do it though, that's all I know. We were fighting for our existence, that's why we won. But it must never happen again. If it doesn't, then perhaps it will have been worthwhile. But only if it never happens again."

Amnon of Kibbutz Gat recalls going into the battle area: "There, lying next to each other, were our dead and their dead. Suddenly you realized that they were all the same."

The concept of tohar haneshek, "fighting clean," is discussed at length, as the young soldiers give examples of tending enemy wounded or helping civilians. At Kibbutz Givat Hashlosha there is the following exchange:

Yigal: You can talk about arms being justly borne, you can talk about them being defensive weapons, but you can't talk about them being pure. What can be pure about them, when there is blood and ... ?

Hillel: But the fact that the war was fought for some principle makes it pure, in which case the arms are pure too. Of course there is dirt wherever you go. The borderline between murder and killing in war is very blurred.

In a conversation at Mishmar Hasharon, Avinoam talks about

"getting the better of your savage instincts" in war. "Not all of us are capable of this. Those who aren't behave in a barbaric manner, but despite the fact that we are fighting for our lives we fight decently and morally, suppressing the sadism and the instinct to kill that is in all of us . . . In my opinion peace is the first thing to strive for, and it precedes love of one's country."

Although the conversations in *The Seventh Day* took place immediately after the 1967 war, the question of the newly occupied territories had already surfaced as a controversial issue. Author Amos Oz, one of the interviewers, quotes the mother of a fallen soldier from his own kibbutz. "The whole of the Western Wall [of the Temple in Jerusalem] isn't worth Micha's little finger, as far as I am concerned." And Oz replies, "If what you are telling me is that we fought for our existence, then I would say that it *was* worth Micha's little finger. But if you tell me that it was the Wall we fought for, then it *wasn't* worth his little finger. Say what you like — I do have a feeling for those stones — but they are only stones. Micha was a person. If dynamiting the Western Wall would bring Micha back to life, then I'd say, blow it up."

Asher of Kibbutz Yifat declares, "Jerusalem is ours; it's got to be ours because I conquered it and I had every right to do so, because I didn't start the war. Everyone knows that Israel didn't want territorial gains . . ."

Maybe then. But I am not sure how many people remember that in 1983, sixteen years after the war. Today the country is split half and half over retention of the occupied territories, but back in 1967 there was a mad rush to visit the West Bank, Gaza, Sinai, and the Golan Heights, "before we give them back." It was generally assumed that Israel would return the areas in exchange for peace, but the Arab states put the brakes on that one. At the Arab summit in Khartoum after the Six Day War, it was resolved: No peace, no negotiations, and no recognition of Israel — the three famous nos of Khartoum.

It encouraged the fatalistic attitude of Eli from Kibbutz Yifat.

"I cannot see any solution to the whole problem. That's our life, that's how we've got to live, and that's how we have to educate our children, and perhaps we should have a few more children. There will be another war — it's out of our hands."

With the wisdom of hindsight we can say that the Six Day War was a Pyrrhic victory, for it changed the nature of the state. At the time I wrote to a friend: "It rather frightens me. Up to now we have been living in a cozy little cottage, familiar and intimate. Now it is as if we have moved into a great castle, with long, gloomy corridors and gigantic halls."

Israel went to war to defend itself and ended up with territories many times larger than its own. Dayan was being honest when he declared on the outbreak of war, "Our aim is not conquest, but to safeguard our security." However, once Israel had occupied the Golan Heights in Syria, the West Bank of the Jordan, the Gaza Strip, and the Sinai Peninsula, it wasn't so simple.

The Arab states did not make things any easier by their resolute refusal to deal with Israel. Their attitude strengthened the voices of those in Israel who were beginning to say that the newly conquered land should be kept. Ben-Gurion stated, soon after the war, that — with the exception of Jerusalem, Israel's eternal capital, and the Golan Heights, from which the Syrians had shelled Galilee — the territories should be returned in exchange for peace, but the Arabs were not buying. In a memorable phrase, Moshe Dayan said he was "waiting for the phone call from Amman or Cairo." It never came.

For the next few years Israel carried out a policy that was a combination of the ideas of two lifelong rivals: Moshe Dayan and Yigal Allon. Allon had been the outstanding general of the 1948 war; Dayan, BG's favorite, had been the chief of staff in 1956 and the defense minister in 1967.

Dayan was actually in charge of the new territories and he believed in flexibility, pragmatism, solving problems day by day, and keeping all options open. The more systematic Allon came out with a plan, the principle of which was maximum territory (except in Sinai) and security, minimum Arab population. Thus Israel would keep the Golan, a strip of land along the Jordan River, some of the West Bank south of Jerusalem, and northern Sinai. The heavily populated parts of the West Bank and most of the Gaza Strip would be returned to Arab rule — probably Jordanian. Although Dayan blocked the adoption of the Allon plan as official policy, over the next years official settlement policy began to be implemented more or less along the lines of the plan.

In the territories Dayan pursued a combination of a strong policy against resistance and a liberal day-to-day administration. The local municipalities continued to function, there was little interference in the daily lives of the Arab inhabitants, the bridges across the river Jordan were left open, and people and goods were allowed to pass in both directions. At the same time political organization was not permitted, those suspected of supporting insurrection were deported, and the houses of terrorist suspects were blown up. Where the courts were unable to act, administrative detention was used, albeit sparingly.

Tendencies that had always been present in Israeli society came to the fore. Large numbers of West Bank and Gaza Arabs came to work in Israel, providing a pool of cheap labor. This benefited the occupied territories economically but had a degenerating effect on the old Labor Zionist principle of self-labor. Already larger, Israel became richer and more vulgar. The race for consumer goods and the tendency to ape the affluent societies of the West became more pronounced. In command of such sweeping territories, Israelis became more self-confident, but their confidence gravitated toward arrogance.

The IDF soldiers who garrisoned the West Bank and Gaza behaved for the most part with a measure of humanity and decency, but, almost imperceptibly, they began to feel themselves the masters. Since 1948 Arabs in Israel had been, to an extent, second-class citizens, but at least they were citizens. They had the vote and they elected their representatives to the Knesset.

Now a whole population had no democratic self-expression. Richard Crossman, a British Labour politician and a good friend of Israel, wrote a public letter to Foreign Minister Abba Eban in which he said, "The Arabs can stand a decade of Israeli occupation — the Israel you and I believe in can't."

Crossman was right. After the initial rush to see the territories "before we give them back," an increasing number of Israelis began to believe that they had every right to retain the new areas. Today, teen-agers who will be going into the army in two years' time have never known an Israel without the West Bank, Gaza, and the Golan.

Soon after the 1967 war partisan settlement projects were initiated by nationalistic circles to pressure the government into wide-scale Jewish settlement in the West Bank. At first these were resisted by the Labor government, but some of them turned into accomplished facts. The Kefar Etzion group of villages, south of Jerusalem, and the town of Kiryat Arba, next to Hebron, were originally "illegal" settlements by unauthorized groups.

One of the most significant developments was a new activism among religious nationalist youth, who played a leading part in these settlement attempts. Hitherto, religious Zionists had been in the minority. Many religious Jews opposed (and still oppose) Zionism on the grounds that it is an impertinent anticipation of the Messiah. Religious Zionism, such as it was, had been moderate and even defensive.

Now a new militant religious Zionism, which proclaimed that the Six Day War had ushered in the first stage of the Messianic age, was born.

It all began (unknown to most of us) at the Mercaz Harav yeshiva, a religious seminary in Jerusalem. On the occasion of Israel's Independence Day, about a month before the Six Day War, Rabbi Zvi Yehuda Kook, the son of a much-respected former chief rabbi, preached a sermon in which he bemoaned the fact that the Jews were living in what he called a "truncated land of Israel," without Hebron, Shechem (Nablus), and Jericho.

The sermon, according to an eyewitness account, "evoked a flood of weeping, for we had transgressed and forgotten." Only a month later, Hebron, Nablus, and Jericho were in Jewish hands and many of his audience became convinced that Rabbi Kook was a "divinely inspired prophet."

These new religious activists made no claim to either logic or rationality. Quite the reverse. One of their early pamphlets contains the following passage:

"Being practical has never been the Jewish answer. The Hasmoneans were not practical. They were idealists. They were committed. They made sacrifices. They overcame the superpowers of their day. We, their heirs, must pursue this same 'impossible' course . . . We will — with God's help — prevail."

Their knowledge of history was less profound than their belief and faith. The Hasmonean revolt of the second century B.C. was a failure and almost ended in disaster. Its leader, Judah the Maccabee, did indeed win some great military victories, but he was eventually killed and defeated. It fell to his pragmatic younger brother, Jonathan, to make compromises, forge local alliances, and save the Jewish nation from extinction. Judah was a "committed idealist," but if his story teaches anything, it is that idealism and commitment are not enough.

The leaders of the new religious nationalism have little patience with such sophistry, and their fervent conviction won wide-scale support among the people. When Israel was surprised by the Egyptians and the Syrians in the Yom Kippur War and suffered initial setbacks in the conflict, the nation was shaken to its foundations. If many Israelis felt that it was the retention of the territories that caused the war, others worried about what would have happened if Israel had been attacked across its former borders.

In the period of uncertainty and confusion after the war, the assurance of the nationalists, and particularly the certainty of the religious nationalists, won even wider support. They founded a movement called *Gush Emunim*, "movement of believers."

Rabbi Moshe Levinger, one of the leaders of Gush Emunim, does not appear to be a charismatic figure. Awkward and shy in conversation, with a strange smile that comes over as a grimace, he gropes for words and is slow to come to the point. But his single-minded devotion to the cause of the Land of Israel has won him the adoration of his followers. A veteran of many unauthorized attempts at settlement, he was the founder of Kiryat Arba, led the resistance to the withdrawal from Sinai — carried out under the Israel-Egypt peace treaty — and has now led Jewish settlement into the very heart of the Arab town of Hebron.

When Henry Kissinger was negotiating disengagement along the Suez Canal after the 1973 war, there was a demonstration outside the prime minister's office in Jerusalem by those who opposed an Israeli pullback. The few hundred demonstrators were standing quietly with their placards until the bearded, bespectacled rabbi appeared on the scene.

Emitting an anguished howl, the redoubtable Levinger quite literally rent his garments, tearing his jacket and shirt as a sign of mourning. He then lay down on the ground and his followers, as if mesmerized, did the same. When the police came to pick him up and carry him away, he struggled furiously, and his followers, many of them with babies in their arms, joined in the fracas, moaning, "The rabbi, the rabbi."

I was covering the demonstration for the radio and mentioned to the sound engineer, an intelligent, rational man, my horror that babies and children were being dragged into the fight. His answer surprised me. "They will grow up with values; they will believe in something." His response was typical of a remarkable number of Israelis whose faith in the country had been shattered by the war and who were searching for something to believe in. Those of us who tried to argue rationally found that the complexity of our assertions was at a disadvantage when set against the blind faith and utter certainty of the Gush.

The scene in front of the prime minister's office was repeated many times at numerous settlement points in the occupied territories. The Labor government was trying to implement settlement along the lines of the Allon plan, but it was finding it increasingly difficult to resist Gush pressure.

Gush Emunim became more activist. The youngsters with their knitted skullcaps filled our television screens and dominated the media. A young religious moderate put it this way: "I am opposed to the Gush politically, but they have presented an integrated religious Zionism. Until now, religion was in the synagogue and Zionism was in the army. Judaism had become departmentalized. The Gush points to a way of Zionist fulfillment and it has great attractions for many."

Pragmatism, says Levinger in his slurred, hesitant Hebrew, is not enough. God gave the land of Israel to the Jews for their mission, and they could carry out this mission only if they were rooted in the soil of their land. He is impatient with any suggestion that the Jews should be satisfied with a part of the land. "I would no more suggest cutting off parts of the land than I would suggest the amputation of healthy limbs," he told me.

Democracy is irrelevant to Levinger, who believes that the Jewish national renaissance is more important. Democracy, he maintains, cannot vote away Zionism. He dismisses the argument that it is worth sacrificing parts of the land for peace. "Would we agree to peace on condition we stopped Jewish immigration?" he demands. The integrity of the land is more important than peace, he says. "In any case," he adds, "when we build a real Jewish society based on the Torah, the whole world will have true peace. We have something to say to the world, but we can only say it here."

I remind Levinger that there is another people living in the land. The Arabs, the Palestinians, also regard the land as theirs. "The Torah commands us to love mankind," he intones. This includes the Arabs, he emphasizes. The Arabs are residents and have full civil rights but not political rights. It is a Jewish state.

Troublemakers have to be dealt with, he warns. Stone throwers must be punished. He wants fines increased, jail sentences made longer, and the death sentence for murder. "Spare the rod and spoil the child." He quotes Solomon's proverb with approval — almost with relish. Levinger believes in coexistence, but it is clear he envisages something like that of the rider and his horse.

Many of the West Bank settler-activists are not religious. Lawyer Eliakim Haetzni lives in Kiryat Arba in a small apartment, where he is surrounded by Arab coffee pots and rugs from the Hebron market. He speaks fluent Arabic and makes a genuine personal effort toward coexistence. He says adamantly that Jews can live together with Arabs in the Land of Israel, "But the guns must be in Jewish hands — otherwise we perish." Arab society is based on violence, he avers, so the Jews must be in control. He angrily denies that this is a racist point of view. "I did not say that Arabs as people are inherently violent but that Arab *society* is based on violence. Show me one Arab nation that is not," he challenges.

He recalls that before the Six Day War, some Jews in Israel bought poison, so they would be ready to commit suicide in case Israel lost the war. "From that moment on," he tells me, "I became convinced that it would be suicidal to hand back territory. Even before the war broke out, I had been converted to expansionism."

Nevertheless, Haetzni regards himself as a dove, on the ground that he is prepared to compromise about "those parts of the Land of Israel" east of the Jordan River. "The so-called Kingdom of Jordan does not belong to that parvenu from the Hejaz [Hussein]!"

He is prepared for a Palestinian sovereignty in Jordan, but he demands that Jews have the right to settle there. It is a fair compromise, he thinks: Jewish sovereignty west of the river, with Arab towns and villages; Arab sovereignty east of the river, with Jewish towns and villages.

It sounds reasonable to me, I tell him, but wouldn't it have a more practical chance of success if we drew the border a little to the west of the Jordan, giving the Palestinians most of the West Bank also? No, he retorts. Judea and Samaria are the heartland of Israel.

"What are you talking about, compromise?" demands Hanan Porat, another Gush leader, when I tell him about Haetzni's statement. "We are not prepared to compromise on *anything!*"

With his finely chiseled features, stocky frame, and worker's hands, Porat looks like a young kibbutznik, which is precisely what he is. A paratroop veteran of the wars of 1967 and 1973, he personifies the new-style religious Jew, his knitted skullcap perched jauntily on his head. He lives at Kefar Etzion, south of Jerusalem, but I met him at his Knesset office. In parliament he represents the right-wing *Tehiya* (Renaissance) party, which is more or less the parliamentary voice of Gush Emunim.

Our conversation was interrupted by numerous phone calls. Porat spoke to government officials with an easy assurance. He discussed practical matters: loans, buildings, roads, electricity, water. I was reminded of the young kibbutz leaders of the 1950s; Hanan Porat, the former rebel, has become a part of Israel's new power elite.

"We are not prepared to compromise on anything," he repeats. "Not Jordan, not South Lebanon, or the rebuilding of the Temple in Jerusalem." He sees my eyebrows go up at this, for, to rebuild the Temple, we would first have to dismantle two of Islam's holiest sites, the El-Aksa Mosque and the Dome of the Rock. "Yes, indeed," he says, "and I want the world to know that a 'madman' like me is saying this!" He smiles, but his steely blue eyes blaze with conviction.

"What about the Arabs? The Arabs will join us if we build a real Jewish society worthy of the name. Don't talk to me about demography. Do you know how many children Levinger has? Thirteen. And how many Hanan Porat has? Eight — and I'm still young. It's not by chance. I don't regard my wife as a childbearing machine, but we believe in a pure, Jewish family life. We will attract God-fearing Jews from all over the world.

"We want to set up a counter to all this perversion. Look at the pornography displayed in Tel Aviv. It's worse than New York — and in New York it is the Jews who are the leaders of all this

avant-garde rubbish. We Jews are extremists. We are either totally degraded or divinely inspired.

"We will achieve it all: the entire Land of Israel, the Temple,
everything."

If I didn't have a cassette recording, I might doubt my memory,
but Porat means every word. He comes across with white-hot
conviction.

I almost wish that Porat and his friends could rebuild their Temple, for, if they did so and the Messiah did not appear, their whole
absurd edifice would come crumbling down. I am reminded of
Shabtai Zvi, the "false messiah" of the seventeenth century. A
young Jewish mystic from Turkey proclaimed himself the Messiah and inspired thousands of Jews, promising to lead them to
the Promised Land. Eventually he was thrown into a Turkish
dungeon and, threatened with torture, he converted to Islam.
The faith of his followers collapsed like a punctured balloon.

Ultimately it must happen with Gush Emunim; yet I wonder
how much harm they will do before it happens.

Apart from giving Israel more territory with a disenfranchised
Arab population and spawning Gush Emunim, the Six Day War
also launched the rehabilitation of Menachem Begin. Until then
he had been not so much the leader of the opposition as a political
outcast. Ben-Gurion, who coined the term "without Herut and
the Communists," so disapproved of Begin that he would not
mention him by name, referring to him in the Knesset as "the
member who sits on the right of Dr. Bader."

Begin had been the leader of the *Irgun Zvai Leumi*, a dissident
underground movement, which operated independently from the
Labor movement's Haganah defense organization. More radical
than the Haganah, it had carried out a number of operations of
which BG disapproved.

In 1946, when the British mandate authorities were preventing
the immigration of Jewish Holocaust survivors to Palestine, the
Irgun blew up the King David Hotel, where the British admin-

istrative headquarters was situated, with the loss of ninety-one British, Arab, and Jewish lives. Two years later, when Jerusalem was under siege by the Arabs, the Irgun, together with another dissident group, stormed the village of Deir Yassin on the outskirts of the capital, killing two hundred fifty Arabs, many of them women and children.

When the Irgun tried to land an arms ship, the *Altalena*, during the 1948 war, BG ordered it to be blown out of the water and the country teetered on the brink of civil war.

When elections were held for the first Knesset, Begin converted his movement into the Herut party and contested the election democratically, but still BG did not forgive him. The hatred between the two men increased when Begin led a mob in violent demonstrations against an agreement to accept reparations from West Germany.

But in 1967, on the eve of war, Begin was co-opted into a National Unity government, with BG's approval, and the two men shook hands. Even before the Six Day War, Begin had moved to broaden his power base, linking up with the centrist Liberal party to form a right-wing bloc. The Gahal alliance, made up of the small businessmen who supported the Liberals and Begin's nationalist Herut, provided Israel with a proper opposition for the first time, but they were still a long way from challenging the Labor hegemony.

It was a situation unlike that in any other country. The Labor movement, with its kibbutzim and moshavim, its Histadrut trade union confederation, its powerful Bank *Hapoalim* (Workers' Bank), its Histadrut holding company, *Hevrat Ovdim*, which owned much of the country's industry, was the establishment.

Gahal was the conservative opposition, but it soon began to attract the authentic working class — the masses of oriental Jewish immigrants who had come to Israel in the 1950s and became a majority of the nation.

They came from all the nations of the Middle East and there are enormous differences of culture and background among them;

they have collectively become known as the *Edot Hamizrach*, the "Eastern ethnic groups." By no means did all of them support Begin, but he attracted the majority of their votes, a majority that increased over the years.

It was only partially Begin's hard-line nationalism that attracted the Edot. His main appeal was that he, like them, was an outsider. In 1977 he was the outsider who had made it. Not that his nationalism was a disadvantage, but Begin was most popular among the North African Jews, who were treated best by their host countries, and far less popular among the Jews of Iraq, where there were frequent anti-Jewish outrages and pogroms.

Zionism was basically a movement of European Jews, and the Labor establishment of Israel is overwhelmingly European in origin. Jews emigrated from Arab lands throughout the last hundred years or so, but they were in a minority.

After the establishment of the State of Israel in 1948, the mainly European Jewish community of six hundred thousand found themselves "invaded" by some seven hundred thousand Jews from Iraq, Iran, Yemen, Egypt, Tunisia, Morocco, and Algeria. About one hundred thousand European Holocaust survivors also arrived in the 1950s, but they found Israeli society less alien to them.

The enormous task of absorbing a community larger than its own was carried out by the infant state with remarkable success: all were fed and housed; ultimately, all were absorbed into the economy and the society. But the old-timers showed a notable lack of sensitivity, the results of which are still evident today, three decades later.

Deputy Prime Minister David Levy, himself an immigrant from Morocco, eloquently described the bitterness of the newcomers of the 1950s in a 1983 biography (*David Levy*, by Arye Avneri). They were less upset by the primitive conditions in which they had to live than by the attitudes they encountered.

He and his family were sent to live in the Jordan Valley development town of Bet Shean, despite having asked to be allowed to join relatives in Beersheba. The family had been reasonably well-off in Morocco, but it lost its possessions on the way to Israel. More important than the loss of their furniture and other personal belongings was the loss of the senior Levy's tools. A carpenter by profession, David Levy's father had hoped to earn an honorable living at his own trade. Too poor to acquire new tools of his own and unable to get work in his profession, the father became depressed and before very long was existing on welfare handouts and the day labor of his children.

"I saw how quickly my father, a man who had always honorably supported his family, quickly turned from an authoritative father into a pathetic social case," Levy told his biographer. Coming from a patriarchal society, the new immigrants found the traditional frameworks shattered and nothing to take their place. On the contrary, in their desire to absorb them into Israel's "modern" society, immigration officials were all too ready to break up families and alter "primitive" lifestyles.

Levy described vividly how he had to fight to get on the truck that took the day laborers to work in the nearby kibbutzim and how he often had to walk home at the end of the day. On one occasion the young Levy organized a strike to compel the kibbutz to supply the workers with cold water to drink in the burning climate of the Jordan Valley. During periods when there was no work, he and his companions were humiliatingly grilled at the local welfare office and asked why they needed "handouts."

In those years there was no time to build permanent housing for the flood of immigrants, and most of them were accommodated in *ma'abarot* (transit camps) in tents or corrugated iron huts. Some of them were still in existence in 1954, when I came to spend a year in Israel. I was appalled at the way people lived. There were often as many as twelve individuals in a hut that measured eighteen feet by six, with toilets outside and water available only from a distant tap. Tables, chairs, and iron beds formed the furniture,

and cupboards were improvised from boxes and crates. Cooking
was done on a kerosene stove and there were quite often accidents
caused by the overcrowding.

Burning hot in the summer, freezing cold and leaky in the
winter, the huts were situated among acres of dust, which turned
into seas of mud in the rainy season.

As many of the ma'abarot, which later became new towns,
were situated in close proximity to the kibbutzim, it was there
that the newcomers were most easily able to find work. Within
the kibbutz movement a big debate ensued. Self-labor was a
sacred principle of kibbutz life, and many kibbutz members were
reluctant to jettison it — even for the sacred task of absorbing
new immigrants. But Ben-Gurion insisted that they had a national, Zionist responsibility to provide work, and for the most
part he had his way.

Perhaps the kibbutzniks spent too much time debating whether
to give the newcomers jobs and too little time considering the
nature of the relationship between employer and employee. But
this is said with the wisdom of hindsight. What in fact happened
was that a master-servant relationship developed between kibbutz and development town, and the resentments still linger.

There was nothing to prevent the immigrants from joining the
kibbutzim, but the highly developed communal lifestyle was not
attractive to them or appropriate to their cultural tradition. Some
joined, but they were a minority.

The most infuriating thing for the new immigrants of the 1950s
was their constantly being told that they should be "grateful."
Grateful for being admitted to Israel, grateful for their primitive
housing conditions, grateful for being given work in the kibbutzim, grateful for being permitted into the "advanced, modern,
enlightened Israeli society."

Most of them did indeed come from countries that are today
described as "developing," but technological backwardness was
brutally confused with cultural backwardness. The Jews from
Iraq and Morocco had a long tradition of learning and a colorful

folk culture. The Israeli host society initially showed no appreciation for the "primitive" culture of the newcomers. It was of course true that many of the more educated and wealthy North Africans went to Canada and France, whereas all the artisan class came to Israel, and this did not improve the situation.

The kibbutz became a particular focus for resentment. In the 1950s many kibbutzim had already become prosperous communities and thriving economic enterprises. It was easier to solve the employment problem for the masses of immigrants by letting them work in the kibbutz fields and factories than to establish new industries for them in the development towns. Israel, with its chronic defense burden, was always short of money for development. But the immigrants saw it differently.

"All the money went to the kibbutzim," I was told by a Moroccan-born Jew who came to the country as a child. "It was done deliberately so that we could work for them and provide a source of cheap labor. We made them rich." He continued, "We were good enough to work in the kibbutz factory, but not good enough to swim in the kibbutz pool."

In the long, hot Israeli summers, the kibbutz swimming pool became a symbol of the difference between the old and the new Israel. The kibbutzniks lived in green villages with mown lawns and trim flower beds, whereas the citizens of the development towns lived in stifling apartments set in a bare, brown landscape. While kibbutz children splashed in the clear, cool water of the kibbutz pool, the development town child played in the dust.

The newcomers did not consider the fact that the green kibbutzim had been brown a few years previously, or that the kibbutzniks had labored hard and long to create their "Gardens of Eden." They saw only the inequity and the hypocrisy of the "so-called Socialist society."

Begin was skillful in exploiting this feeling. As recently as the 1981 election campaign, he described kibbutz members as "arrogant millionnaires, lounging by their swimming pools." He touched a raw nerve and, in the crowd, even the youngsters who had grown up with swimming pools in their towns roared in appreciation.

It is grossly unfair to single out such a hard-working and creative sector of Israeli society as the kibbutzim and accuse them of discrimination. The luxury suburbs of Tel Aviv and the rich neighborhoods of Herzliya and Caesarea are also predominantly European. You don't find many families of the Edot living there, but the kibbutzim, as part of the Labor movement, are a convenient target.

Nor can the kibbutzim entirely escape blame. In some parts of the country, regional schools have been established for both kibbutzim and immigrant moshavim, but in many regions the kibbutzim have preferred to retain an educational exclusivity. Only two years ago, the kibbutzniks pulled their children out of the local regional school, which my own children attended in the Judean hills near Jerusalem. They claimed that they wanted their children to receive an education geared toward communal and pioneering values, but the local villagers, mostly from the Edot, simply regarded them as elitist snobs.

By 1961, when I arrived in Israel to make the country my permanent home, the ma'abarot had been more or less abolished. Some remained as slum areas of the larger towns, but for the most part the Edot seemed to be fully a part of Israeli society. This, however, was a very superficial assessment. The resentment felt almost universally among the Edot and the superiority felt by the European Jews simmered beneath the surface.

Going to live in the new town of Arad, I immediately sensed this feeling and wrote about it in the local town bulletin because I felt it should be brought out into the open. A number of my European fellow citizens rebuked me and told me "not to confuse the color prejudice you knew in England" with the situation in Israel. Two neighbors, immigrants from the 1950s, warmly congratulated me on the article. But it was only when I went to work on the Dead Sea dikes construction project that the full extent of resentment among the Edot became apparent to me.

The Dead Sea is situated in the giant Syrian-African rift, which runs from Syria, down the Jordan and Arava valleys to the Red Sea, and thence to East Africa. Set in a blinding, beige-white desert, the sea is more than a thousand feet below normal sea level.

To the east tower the mauve mountains of Moab and Edom; to the west, the forbidding cliffs of Israel's Judean desert. It is a harsh, inhospitable place, with temperatures reaching well over a hundred degrees in the shade in summer.

The Dead Sea is the most saline in the world, and our project was to build dikes in the sea, dividing it into pans for the extraction of potash, bromine, salt, and other materials. Even at six in the morning the sun burned when we stepped out of the bus, and later in the day the dry and oppressive ovenlike heat hit us like a physical blow.

The majority of the workers came from Arad and the nearby development towns of Yeruham, Dimona, and Beersheba. Most of the administrative workers were of European origin; the outside workers, with the exception of a few former kibbutzniks, came from the Edot.

I worked for a time as the clerk in the heavy equipment office, where the tractor drivers, crane operators, truck drivers, and others came to rest between shifts. From their conversation I quickly learned their perception that the "whites" worked in the air-conditioned offices, whereas the "blacks" labored out in the sun in unbearable temperatures. They were quite sure that the personnel manager (Guttman) and his assistant (Shechter) found jobs for their European buddies, leaving the Moroccans, Tunisians, Iraqis, and Yemenites to work in the sun. The fact that people from the Edot also worked in the offices did not alter this simplistic view.

When, as happened frequently, there were disputes over the time cards and workers were accused of punching their friends' cards to cover up absenteeism or late arrival, the resentment became particularly fierce. They did not really look on me as a European — England and America were the same as far as they were concerned, and I was a "crazy Zionist" for coming to live in Israel — so they spoke quite freely in front of me. Gaston, who hailed from Tunis, told me that he had come to understand the Germans. "If all the European Jews are like Guttman," he said, "the Germans were right to put them in gas chambers."

I tried to explain something of the meaning of the Holocaust to him, but it did not make much of an impression. I managed to find a copy in French of André Schwarz-Bart's *The Last of the Just*. He read it and later took back what he had said. He had not, he explained, realized the enormity of the European Jewish experience. But I don't know how many crazy Zionists were around to distribute copies of Schwarz-Bart's masterpiece. The resentment was powerful, but it remained beneath the surface for a number of years more.

I had come to live in Jerusalem in the early 1970s, when the Black Panther movement was formed in the capital. Deliberately taking its name from the American movement, and encouraged by a number of American immigrant social workers, it was far less radical than its U.S. counterpart. Its leaders had no aspirations toward tearing down the fabric of society. What they wanted was a fair slice of the national cake.

The Panthers soared into the headlines of the national press through a series of public demonstrations. The concept of political demonstrations was new to the Edot people and they were not quite sure how to behave. Most of the police also came from the Edot and they, too, were uncertain. Many of the demonstrations turned violent and elicited considerable public concern, not least from the government, which was then headed by veteran Golda Meir, who quite simply did not understand what was going on.

A Labor party leader from the port city of Ashdod, Shaul Ben-Simhon, himself an immigrant from Morocco, arranged a meeting between a number of young Panther leaders and the prime minister. Introducing them, he jokingly referred to them as "our sometimes nice boys." But when the boys came to speak, they

protested against their situation in the sort of language Golda
was unused to.

Golda Meir was a sincere but narrow-minded Labor-Zionist
ideologue. In the 1950s, while visiting Holocaust survivors at a
ma'abara, she had run into a storm of complaining and rebuked
them for their "lack of gratitude." She was not ethnically prej-
udiced, but she could not bear to hear criticism of the Zionist
achievement.

When she replied to the complaints, she ticked off Ben-Simhon:
"They are not 'nice boys.' Why did you call them that?" The
encounter was televised, and Golda's remarks were broadcast to
the whole nation, which has only one TV channel to watch. The
sentence was to haunt her for the rest of her political life. The
fact that a European prime minister thought that Edot youths
were "not nice boys" would eventually bring Menachem Begin
to power.

After the meeting Golda set up a committee to look into the
problems of disadvantaged youth. It was headed by Dr. Israel
Katz, head of the National Insurance Institute and a man who
had the full confidence of the Panthers. I, together with other
journalists, was invited to hear Katz's presentation of his report
in the prime minister's office. Katz, a small, soft-spoken social
worker, outlined his agenda, which included extra school classes,
special education courses for young soldiers, university prepara-
tory courses for young soldiers who had not managed to matric-
ulate, more clubhouses, budgets for poor neighborhoods, more
vocational schools, and more youth leaders for street gangs.

Much of that program has since been implemented and the
situation has improved, but there is still a long way to go. The
country's elementary schools are more than half populated by
children from the Edot, but the proportion drops in high school,
and in university it is still below 20 percent.

Golda sat impassively through Katz's presentation. She was a
solid presence: strong, square body, determined face with its
prominent nose, gray bun of hair. When it was my turn to ask a

question I stood up and said, "Mrs. Prime Minister, do you see this report as a continuation of what has gone before or a new departure? If the latter, why only now?"

Her dark eyes seemed to burn a hole in me. I could swear I felt an actual jolt and I was pleased to sit down. I had the impression of an immensely powerful personality who fiercely resented my implication that successive Israeli governments had neglected the problem of the Edot.

Her answer was reasonable enough: the country had grown, the economy was larger, immigration was down, there were more resources available than there had been previously. Now it was possible to sort out some of the problems left over from the earlier immigration.

But the memories of the early humiliations will not go away. David Levy told his biographer that the Labor leaders were like the wolf in a fable by La Fontaine: The goat comes to drink at a spring but is told by the wolf that he must not drink because he will pollute the water.

"I will drink after you," suggests the goat. "No," says the wolf, "that won't help, because you polluted it when you drank from it the preceding day." The goat protests that he was not there on the preceding day, at which the wolf suggests it must have been his brother.

"But I don't have a brother," protests the goat.

"Well, it must have been one of your family. In any case I am going to eat you," insists the wolf.

That, claims Levy, is how the Labor party treated him. The exaggeration is obvious, but there is no doubt about his genuine resentment.

Furthermore, the contempt has not disappeared. When he became a cabinet minister, Levy was subjected to a series of tasteless jokes, akin to Polack jokes told in the United States. By his own testimony he was bitterly hurt by the jokes, which, he says, were even passed in notes across the cabinet table. "The prime minister," he informed his biographer, "never told such jokes." Small wonder that for many from the Edot, Begin, the former outsider, became a symbol with whom they could identify.

Searching for a personal angle, I recall my days in Arad. How was I able to win acceptance into the Israeli-born, sabra society? The clue was the youth movement and the kibbutz. I was one of the *hevre*, the "gang," because I had been in a youth movement and had lived at a kibbutz.

In his book, *The Israelis: Founders and Sons*, Amos Elon quotes actor Haim Topol as saying, "I know *everyone* of my age in Israel." What Topol meant was that he knew everyone in the hevre. He was not talking about the daughter of the Moroccan stall holder or the son of the Iraqi bank clerk, or the children of the Georgian street sweeper. He knew the sabras, who spent their summers at kibbutz work camps and their winters hiking in the hills with the youth movement, and later joined the elite combat units of the IDF.

My fellow citizens in Arad often laughed at the Moroccan-accented Hebrew of the former immigrants, but they never laughed at my bad, atrociously English-accented Hebrew.

Begin was clever in capitalizing on the resentment of the Edot against the "youth movement–kibbutz–Histadrut–elite IDF unit–Labor party snobs." There is no question that with Labor regarded as the establishment, Begin's populism made his Likud bloc the party of the lower-paid workers, most of them from the Edot.

"Begin is one of us, he lives in a rented apartment; Peres [the Labor leader] is a capitalist" was a frequently heard refrain.

"He is like a father to us" was another. And there is no doubt that Begin replaced the authoritative father figure of whom they feel Labor deprived them. It also accounts for the terrible anger they felt when they thought he was being insulted by his political opponents. I was once told in Jerusalem's Mahane Yehuda market, "The Labor people teach their children to curse Begin."

Asked why so many of the Edot supported Begin, former Panther leader (and today Communist member of parliament) Charlie Biton replied, "They think he's a Moroccan!" Not so funny as it sounds. An army buddy of mine who hailed from Casablanca once told me in all seriousness that he had heard that Begin's family came to Poland from Morocco. Other friends report similar experiences.

Jules Daniel, a journalist born in Morocco, maintains that the attitude of the European Jews also forced the Edot into an exaggerated nationalistic position. "We were looked on as half-Arabs," he explains. "Our reaction was to prove that we were super-Zionists by taking up an aggressive anti-Arab stance. We wanted to show our patriotic credentials."

All these factors combined to make Begin specially appealing to the Edot, and a new variant emerged to reinforce this feeling. Author Amos Oz, speaking to people in the development town of Bet Shemesh, was told, "You people love the Arabs more than you like us: you want to make us unskilled workers again." It is true that the Labor movement has bemoaned the fact that since the Six Day War much of the unskilled labor in Israel has been done by Arabs from the West Bank and Gaza. The Edot people recall that before this was true, it was they who performed many of the menial tasks. They refuse to believe that the Labor supporters want to return to the traditional value of self-labor; they see it as a simple attempt to turn the clock back and put them back into the unskilled jobs.

Menachem Begin won his first election in 1977 almost by chance. True, he had widened his Herut base by joining with the Liberals. True, the Gush Emunim revival had brought the National Religious party toward a strong nationalist line, making it the natural political ally of his Likud. True, also, that his support among the Edot had grown and that the Edot now formed a higher proportion of the electorate. But all these factors were not enough.

There was great disillusion with Labor, which had ruled for

three decades and was showing the classical signs of both tiredness and the corruption of power. Authoritative figures like Golda Meir and Ben-Gurion had been replaced by the "gray" figures of Shimon Peres and Yitzhak Rabin, who were feuding between themselves, but Labor still won in 1973, even after the Yom Kippur War.

In 1977 there was a "soft option" for disgruntled Labor supporters who could not yet bring themselves to vote for Begin. A centrist movement called the Democratic Movement for Change (DMC) was formed. Headed by former chief of staff Yigael Yadin, a nonpolitical figure who had been associated with Labor, and including a number of Labor defectors, it attracted a remarkable number of votes and put fifteen members into Israel's one-hundred-twenty-member Knesset, mostly at Labor's expense.

Begin, now the head of the largest party, was able to form a coalition with his new allies in the National Religious party. He also co-opted the non-Zionist Orthodox party, which will always go along with any government willing to fund its *yeshivot* — "religious seminaries." This gave him a bare majority, but he later brought in the centrist Democratic Movement for Change, creating a potentially strong government with a stable majority.

Begin did not need Gush Emunim to teach him devotion to the Land of Israel idea. The Revisionist Zionists, the precursors of his Herut movement, had broken away from the mainstream Zionist movement, headed by Labor, in 1921, when the majority accepted "the first partition of the Land of Israel." This was when the British mandate authorities lopped off Transjordan and made Emir Abdulla (Hussein's grandfather) its king. The Herut youth movement, *Betar*, still sings the song "Both Sides of the Jordan" as its anthem. While few take this seriously, Begin and his associates were resolutely opposed to withdrawing from any territory captured in the 1967 war.

Immediately after the 1977 election, Begin went to one of the illegal West Bank settlements of Gush Emunim and declared that it was perfectly legal and that there would be many more.

He further lectured the assembled journalists: "Until now you called this the 'occupied territories'; now I suppose you will start calling them the 'liberated territories.'"

As agriculture minister, Ariel Sharon soon began to keep Begin's promises, driving forward with Jewish settlement on the West Bank, but this was still not an authentic Begin government. The centrist DMC, Moshe Dayan, Ezer Weizman, and — most of all — Anwar Sadat put the brakes on the first administration — Begin-I. Begin was prime minister in 1977, but he really won power only in 1981.

The 1977 campaign was managed for the Likud by Ezer Weizman, a former air force commander and a popular figure. During the campaign, he kept Begin almost out of sight, and after the cabinet was formed he acted as a moderating influence, as minister of defense.

It was a measure of Begin's lack of confidence, after three decades in opposition, that prompted him to appoint the former Labor defense minister, Moshe Dayan, as his foreign minister, but it was also a shrewd move. It not only upset the defeated Labor party, but Dayan was a suitable man to conduct the secret moves toward an accommodation with Egypt, which led to President Sadat's dramatic visit to Jerusalem. The Sadat initiative and the consequent moves toward Camp David and the Israel-Egypt peace treaty kept Begin-I in check.

I wonder whether anyone in human history has been as underestimated as Anwar Sadat. When he succeeded the charismatic Nasser as president of Egypt, he was regarded as a nonentity in Israel, which brusquely ignored his first peace overtures.

When Sadat announced 1973 as his "year of decision," it was treated as a joke in Israel. No one took him seriously, largely because of his slow, hesitant style of speech. He was portrayed as a hashish-smoking dimwit on a satirical television program.

But in October 1973 he launched the Yom Kippur War and gave Israel a nasty shock. The Syrians neared Galilee and the

Egyptians crossed the Suez Canal. Although Israel fought back, taking more territory on the Golan and pushing to within sixty miles of Cairo, the Egyptians retained forces on the eastern side of the canal and won an important psychological victory.

In November 1977, with the same flair that he had shown in war, Sadat launched his peace initiative with a move so spectacular that it left us all rubbing our eyes in disbelief.

I have mentioned the eerie feeling of crossing the border into an Arab country. Israel was not so much cut off from the Arab world as cauterized. For three decades Arab leaders would not even mention Israel's name and the Jewish state did not appear on their maps. They claimed to be in a state of war with the "Zionist entity," and organized a boycott of countries that dared to trade with it. For an Arab leader to announce that he was coming to Jerusalem was, quite simply, incredible.

I remember the discussions at Israel radio about covering the visit. We assumed that the Egyptian president was going to helicopter to the Knesset, deliver his speech, and hightail it out of there with all possible speed. We thought he had shot off his mouth when he said he was prepared to come, and now that Begin had invited him, he would keep his word in as minimal a way as possible. The public at large did not believe he would come at all, but when it became clear that he was actually coming, the mood was one of jubilation.

The day before his visit my wife and I drove north to a kibbutz wedding in Galilee, picking up two hitchhiking soldiers on the way. One was a sabra of European origin: serious, intellectual, wearing glasses. He was keeping his cool: it was early days yet, you did not make peace overnight after three decades of hostility. The other soldier, dark, stocky, clearly from the Edot, was ebullient: Begin will bring us peace, even though everyone said he was a warmonger. It was possible to deal with the Arabs. He knew them only too well from Morocco, where there had been good relations between Arabs and Jews. There would be Israeli experts in Egypt, cooperative enterprises, and, above all, trade.

We were traveling through the West Bank town of Jericho at the time and I asked my wife if she wanted to stop and buy oranges.

"It is no cheaper in Jericho today," cut in the soldier. "Why buy from an Arab when it is just as cheap to buy from a Jew?"

"But what about all that trade?" I expostulated.

"Don't confuse two different things," he retorted sternly.

Sadat meant business. He not only stayed overnight in Jerusalem, in itself a remarkable gesture, but he visited the memorial for victims of the Nazi Holocaust at Yad Veshem, laid a wreath at the memorial of the unknown Israeli soldier, stood at attention for the Israeli national anthem, addressed the Knesset plenum, and met with all the political factions separately.

In his Knesset address Sadat took a tough line, demanding that Israel return all the territory taken in 1967, but he also declared, "There is a place for you in this corner of the world," and dramatically pledged, "No more war!"

Ze'ev, the *Haaretz* cartoonist, summed up the Sadat visit when he drew a picture of the Egyptian president placing the roof on the house of Zionism. Under Ottoman law, which was current in Palestine at the time of early Jewish settlement, a house was recognized as permanent once the roof was up. The settlers always struggled to get the roof on before local Arab villagers had time to resist.

Sadat declared, "Ninety percent of the Middle East problem is psychological and I have broken the psychological barrier." In many ways he was right, but in point of fact he had come just too late. Menachem Begin might be modified by Weizman, Dayan, and the DMC, but he was still Begin. Israel had already gone too far down the road toward Begin-II, even if the second phase of Begin's administration had not yet arrived.

At the news conference winding up his visit, Sadat explained his stand on borders, which was one of no compromise. "Our land is sacred," he declared. Begin intervened to say, "I can respect that view. I also say our land is sacred."

Sadat was talking about Sinai, Begin about the West Bank and Gaza. As a consequence, Sadat's daring initiative, which should have led to a revolution in the Middle East, resulted only in a separate Israel-Egypt peace — a notable achievement, but one that fell short of what might have been accomplished. Once again, as in the past, the extremist element in Israel was helped by the extremist element among the Arabs: the other Arab countries refused to join the peace process. The PLO denounced Sadat's initiative as a "sellout" of the Palestinian cause.

Begin eventually signed the Camp David accords and the Israel-Egypt peace treaty, but he showed little enthusiasm for the peace process. It took thirteen full days of the time of an American president, and the encouragement of Ezer Weizman and Moshe Dayan, to persuade him at Camp David, and Jimmy Carter was compelled to visit the Middle East to see the peace treaty through.

There was local pressure too. It was during this period that a group of three hundred fifty reserve officers and soldiers of the IDF's top combat units wrote to Begin the letter that led to the formation of the Peace Now movement. Peace Now campaigned actively for the peace process and staged the largest-ever peace demonstration in Israel while Begin and his ministers were at Camp David.

Camp David and the peace treaty should have been manifestations of the unity of the country, but somehow Begin is a natural divider. Both agreements were passed by overwhelming majorities of the Knesset, but nearly half of Begin's own Herut movement voted against.

The Knesset debates should have been inspiring highlights of Israeli democracy; however, my strongest memory of them is of snarling arguments and insults traded between the prime minister and his opponents.

Sadat did not want a separate peace between Israel and Egypt. He wanted the treaty to be the start of a peace process that would solve the Palestinian problem as well, and lead to a new era in the Middle East. He thought he had achieved this aim with the

Camp David accords, which spoke of "the legitimate rights of the Palestinians." Jimmy Carter certainly thought he had. So did Moshe Dayan and Ezer Weizman, although Dayan, at least, was convinced that a settlement could be achieved without an independent Palestinian state. Menachem Begin thought otherwise. It soon became apparent that he had in no way given up Israel's claim to sovereignty over the West Bank and Gaza, and Dayan and Weizman resigned in fairly quick succession.

Begin's talent for divisiveness reached a climax in the 1981 election campaign, the most violent in Israel's history. This time no one kept the prime minister hidden and he animated huge crowds, predominantly from the Edot, with demagogic oratory. The man who had signed a peace treaty with Israel's largest neighbor, Egypt, seemed far more concerned to utter threats against those who were still at war with Israel, the Syrians and the PLO, based in Lebanon.

"Yanosh and Raful are waiting for you," he shouted, and the crowd roared its appreciation. (Yanosh and Raful were the nicknames of the IDF head of Northern Command and the chief of staff.) He also sent the air force to bomb the Iraqi nuclear reactor in Baghdad, prompting the bitter jest from Labor veterans that "half a dozen kibbutznik pilots got more votes for Begin than thousands of kibbutznik campaigners got for the Labor party."

The resentment of the Edot against the Labor establishment was already there, and Begin stirred the pot of hatred with his crack about "millionnaires lounging by their swimming pools." There had always been resentment in some development towns, but this time even a town like Kiryat Shmona, which had previously maintained good relations with the surrounding kibbutzim thanks to the farsighted attitude of some of the local kibbutz members who worked as psychologists, social workers, and youth leaders in the town, was the center for an unprecedented ugly campaign of incitement.

The local branch of the Likud put out a pamphlet depicting the kibbutzniks as ravening monsters coming to Kiryat Shmona at election time to tear the local inhabitants to pieces. Labor party rallies were broken up violently; the party's leaders were shouted down and physically roughed up. An old Labor veteran from a moshav, who appeared on a Labor election broadcast, had her greenhouses smashed.

Begin was helped by the skillful financial manipulation of his finance minister, who cut taxes before the election and flooded the market with imported consumer goods. He was also given a boost by a veteran political colleague who claimed he had discovered a new energy process that would solve the world's fuel problems and "make the Arab oil sheiks drink their oil." The claim turned out to be totally spurious, but by then the election was long over.

However, it was mainly Begin's oratory, and the polarization it achieved, that swept him into office for a second time. He only just made it, and he might never have done so if not for a ghastly blunder on the part of Labor, which indicates that they left themselves wide open to Begin's incitement of the Edot.

At an election eve rally in Tel Aviv, an entertainer named Dudu Topaz, livening up the throng in advance of the political speeches, said, "You here are the real Israel, the decent Israel — not the *chach-chachim* of the Likud, who don't serve in the army, or who, if they do, are only gate guards."

The word *chach-chach*, slang for "North African immigrant," was bad enough, but it was his stereotyping of the men of the Edot as gate guards that was really fatal. "They do not serve in the elite units like you wonderful youth movement and kibbutz kids do," he was in effect saying.

The following night Begin got full mileage out of the blunder. "A certain Mr. Topaz last night denigrated the *chach-chachim*," he said. "I have been told that it refers to our brethren from the Edot. Let me tell Mr. Topaz that all Israelis, all Jews, orientals, Europeans, all of them are war heroes, heroes of our people!"

Even then Begin only just made it, but the margin was enough for him to form his second administration — Begin-II — which would later launch the Lebanon war.

The re-elected Begin did something he had hesitated to do previously: he appointed Ariel Sharon as his minister of defense. One can only speculate about his motives. Sharon's career was an open book. He was known to be unscrupulous, dishonest, rash, and impulsive — hardly the qualities one looks for in a defense minister. But Begin, having agreed to return the entire Sinai Peninsula to Egypt, for which he was criticized even by the Labor party, was keen to prove his patriotic credentials. Furthermore, the last part of Sinai — the part that contained Jewish settlements — was still to be returned. The superhawk, Sharon, could be counted on to execute the painful process with the requisite cunning and ruthlessness. Ultimately, one can state simply that Sharon had the courage of Begin's convictions.

Gush Emunim spearheaded the resistance to handing back the last part of Sinai. The youthful activists in their knitted skullcaps flooded into the peninsula and established "settlements" especially for the purpose of resisting withdrawal. It was an utter perversion of the traditional Zionist settlement ethic, but it won a measure of support. The Gush was joined by the genuine Sinai settlers. Some were people who had lived in Sinai for more than a decade and were horrified at having to vacate their homes and farms. Others, less scrupulous, thought they could make a lot of money from compensation.

The Likud government did not discourage this idea. If Sinai had to be given back, at least a precedent would be established for sky-high compensation. Whatever the political, religious, Zionist, and security considerations are regarding the West Bank, the precedent of Sinai compensation has ensured that it will be prohibitively expensive to dismantle the Jewish settlements there. As someone cynically remarked, "Even the U.S. economy won't be able to stand a withdrawal from the West Bank!"

President Sadat's tragic assassination was viciously exploited by those in extremist circles, who used it as an additional argument against withdrawing from the remainder of Sinai. The very people who had denigrated the Egyptian president as a cynical opportunist suddenly discovered that he was an honorable man. But now that he was gone, his successors could not be trusted to carry out the terms of the peace treaty.

To their credit, Begin and Sharon did not take this line, but the evacuation was conducted amid scenes of farce and tragedy. The antiwithdrawal activists saw tragedy in the abandoning of Jewish settlements; however, the real tragedy was the violent clashes that occurred between the activists and the young IDF soldiers sent to evict them by force. It was one of the most disreputable episodes in modern Israeli history, and the violence and polarization that emerged were later to be felt increasingly, as the Lebanese war dragged on and on and on.

The Sinai debacle behind him, Begin flexed his nationalist muscles. The promulgation of the Golan Heights Law, which extended Israeli law to the Golan, did nothing to consolidate Israel's hold on the territory. It merely antagonized the formerly friendly Druze inhabitants of the region — not to mention the United States and most of the world.

And so, my readers, we have arrived back in June of 1982. Menachem Begin stands at the head of a coalition of his traditional nationalist Zionists, the new Messianic Zionists of Gush Emunim, and the disaffected masses of the Edot. He has named Ariel Sharon, the most extreme example of the ruthless element in the IDF, defense minister. He has a chief of staff of the same ilk.

The old Israel is still around, "the Israel we have seen," but it is a new Israel, the Israel of Menachem Begin, Begin-II — "not the Israel we have seen in the past" — which is dominant. The stage is set, the army is ready to march. It needs only someone to pull the trigger, and the trigger is pulled on June 3 in London by a gang of Palestinian dissidents.

3
A Nation Divided

The war in Lebanon, different from all of Israel's other wars, split the country down the middle and polarized Israeli society as never before. In launching an aggressive war — and one that turned out to be a disaster — Menachem Begin's government squandered the moral reserve, the willingness to fight, and if necessary die, for the existence of the Jewish nation.

I don't believe the reserve is exhausted. If this country again found itself in a life-and-death struggle, the Israel Defense Forces, backed by the people, would perform as valiantly as in the past, but after the Lebanon war, it is going to be that much harder. The Shukis, Dorons, Yigals, Dudus, and Avis are much more suspicious. They have been pushed dangerously near their limit.

After the Nazi Holocaust, many survivors preferred to flee from their Jewish destiny to seek sanctuary in America, South Africa, or Australia, but those who came to Israel gathered themselves as if for a supreme effort to ensure their survival. There was, so they told themselves, no alternative but to fight for their existence. Indeed, the term *ain brera*, "no alternative," became a sort of Israeli national motto. In 1948 it was regarded as the Jews' secret weapon.

Prime Minister Begin and others disputed the traditional wisdom that all our wars had been wars of no alternative, and, historically, they may have been correct. In 1956 and 1967 Israel had taken the initiative, but only when it believed itself to be mortally threatened. With the advantage of hindsight, it might be said that the Sinai Campaign and the Six Day War could have been avoided, but at the time Israelis felt that they were fighting because they had no choice.

Had the Lebanon war been confined to the original, limited aims, I do not believe that the opposition would have been more than marginal. Possibly the government could even have gotten away with a larger operation, had it been more successful, less costly in lives, and less immoral. But the Lebanon war proved costly, ugly, and increasingly unpleasant. Although the katyushas were removed — for the time being — from the northern settlements and the Palestine Liberation Organization removed from Beirut, the "new order" in Lebanon proved to be an illusion, and more Israelis than ever before, except in time of full-scale war, were being killed day by day. The Palestinian problem, as long as Begin's policy remained in force, was as intractable as ever. The Israel Egypt peace treaty became a frigid state of no war. The demand to pull the IDF out of the Lebanese entanglement reached the highest levels of government.

Yitzhak Shamir, then Israel's foreign minister, said in a speech that Israel did not need a peace movement "because all Israelis want peace." Even the most fatuous statements often contain a grain of truth. There is a very widespread longing for peace in Israel. Even in the case of the Lebanon war, the country did not march off to war "with hobnailed boots crashing out the rhythm of marching songs," and all our national leaders, from David Ben-Gurion to Begin, have always stressed their desire for peace.

Many countries have peace movements, but only Israel's is called Peace Now. The name reflects the impatience of its young members with the older generation, which talked about peace but was not prepared to make sufficient sacrifices or take sufficient risks. Peace Now is clear about which risks and which sacrifices it thinks the nation should take. Thousands of stickers and pamphlets proclaim "Peace is greater than Greater Israel."

The original letter of the three hundred fifty officers and soldiers of the reserve was not supposed to launch a movement. It was conceived at the time as a one-time protest, a call to the prime minister to stop his foot-dragging over the peace initiative started by Sadat.

"A government policy that leads to continued rule over one million Arabs is liable to change the Jewish democratic nature of the state," they wrote, "and would make it difficult for us to identify with the basic direction of the State of Israel. The strength of the IDF lies in the identification of its soldiers with the course of the state." If only the prime minister had heeded the implied warning when he decided to launch the war in Lebanon!

The letter evoked such an overwhelming response that a full-scale protest movement, the largest and most effective that this country had ever seen, emerged. Up to this point, the street had been dominated by Gush Emunim. The demonstrations were carried out by the religious youths and they had had a clear field. Now the Gush was served notice that large numbers of young people did not go along with its nationalist line.

Peace Now was an overwhelmingly sabra movement: pugnacious, pragmatic, unsentimental. The members were not prepared to wait for either the Messiah or the millennium. Now that Sadat had come to Jerusalem and declared "no more war," peace was a practical option, and they wanted it *now*.

Young Israelis had first taken to the streets in large numbers to protest about the Yom Kippur War, and their demonstrations eventually led to the resignation of Golda Meir and Moshe Dayan. At the beginning the protests were about Israel's unpreparedness for war and the failure to mobilize the reserve in time, which led to initial setbacks and a high number of casualties. But the young soldiers also began to ask themselves whether the Yom Kippur War could not have been avoided.

Avshalom Vilan, one of the leaders of Peace Now, told me that he had returned from a trip abroad just before the 1973 war and "two weeks later I found myself in the hell of the northern Suez front." He lost his best friend in that war and was fired with a burning determination never again to take part in a war that he felt could be prevented.

Vilan is a member of Kibbutz Negba, a Negev communal village, which heroically resisted the Egyptian advance into the new State of Israel in 1948. Having grown up in the tradition of self-defense, Vilan had volunteered for one of the IDF's elite combat units. I spoke to Vilan in the cafeteria at the Hebrew University, on Mount Scopus in Jerusalem, where he is now a student.

"Okay, so we lost," he said of the Lebanon war. "We tried to prevent the war and we failed. We opposed it and it continued, but at least Peace Now exists, pointing to an alternative way for Israel."

When Vilan was called up, it had not occurred to him to refuse to go. He had answered the call and fought hard. "This is an Israeli movement," he noted. "You can't compare it to the American peace movement, where they burned draft cards. Israel is a small country and it has to defend itself. When we are mobilized, we go and fight; when we are demobilized, we do everything we can to oppose the war by political means."

One of the older supporters of Peace Now is Mordechai Bar-On, a former chief education officer of the IDF. He says it is not surprising that the Israeli peace movement is spearheaded by former members of the IDF combat units. "After all, they know better than anyone what war is all about."

When security was the central problem of the country, Bar-On explained, he had made the army his career, serving as Moshe Dayan's aide in the Sinai Campaign before going on to his other task. "Now, since the Sadat initiative, there is a chance for a genuine peace and peace is the best possible guarantee for our survival," he said.

Peace Now is a sober, middle-of-the-road movement, operating by consensus. It is for territorial compromise, against further

Jewish settlement in the West Bank, for talks with the Palestinians, but there is no consensus opinion on the precise nature of a settlement of the problem. It is a one-issue movement, which does not take a stand on other political and social matters. It simply takes the position that continued occupation of Gaza and the West Bank is harmful to the Zionist cause and will lead to more conflict. It is not really the obverse of Gush Emunim, because it hews faithfully to a democratic process, whereas the Gush is prepared to fight majority opinion by direct action. Gush Emunim says that the Land of Israel is more important than democracy; Peace Now does not say the same about its beliefs.

Although most of Peace Now's members opposed the Lebanon war from the first shot, the idea of refusing to serve was never brought up in the movement forums. Furthermore, with most of its members on the front line, it held off initially from protest demonstrations. The soldiers passed back the message that with the guns still firing, protests would be misinterpreted. This prohibition, however, lasted only until the first cease-fire. From then on the protests grew in size and conviction. Peace Now, though it was joined by many other groups, which sprang up on an ad hoc basis — for example, Soldiers against Silence — remained the mass movement, the centrist stream, the authentic voice of the Israeli liberal conscience.

The siege of Beirut, the bombing, the civilian casualties, the high mortality rate among IDF troops, the misleading by the government, the imprisonment of five thousand Palestinians at the Ansar detention camp near Tyre all became, at different times, the focus of protest.

Israel is a small country and feels its casualties keenly. It is very rare for a war to pass without everyone's being affected by having several acquaintances and a few intimate friends or relatives killed or wounded. The elite combat units, which pay the heaviest price, are made up to a great extent of kibbutz children, and when a kibbutz son or member dies, the whole community goes into mourning.

As in previous wars, the papers were full of black-bordered pictures of handsome young men. Although my son, Etan, had served in the Litani operation, this was my first real war as a parent. I have to testify that the grief I felt at the pictures and the radio announcements was always tempered by a feeling of relief: the relief that my son was not among the casualties.

Many Israeli children have grown up without fathers and there are all too many young war widows in Israel, but for some reason a special status has been reserved for the "bereaved parent." Possibly this is because the widow and the fatherless child have their lives before them: the widow often manages to marry again and the child to acquire a stepfather. For the mother and father of the fallen soldier, it is as if their life's purpose is destroyed. Somehow their grief seems stronger than anyone else's. There have been several cases of parents who died shortly after their sons fell in battle, through the lack of will to go on living. And there have been instances of parental suicides after bereavement in war.

Despite this, in previous wars most Israeli parents adopted heroic, even stoic attitudes, proud of their fallen sons and feeling that their sacrifice had enabled the nation to continue on its path.

One of the most famous documents to come out of our wars was "A letter to the daughters of Israel" written by Naomi Zorea, wife of former IDF General Meir Zorea. Having lost one son in the Six Day War and a second in the Yom Kippur War, Naomi Zorea found strength in the thought that her sons had died so that others might live.

"What is the purpose of all this bloodshed; are this soil and the stones of the Wall worth so many Isaac-sacrifices?" she asks. And she answers herself without ambivalence: "We have had and shall have no alternative." She goes on to describe her husband and son coming home from the war for a short leave and a family picnic. "Yes, the terrible price was worthwhile, if it means that Jewish grandchildren, children and parents, and grandparents will be able to bathe peacefully, even if only for a short time, in their pool in the middle of fields of cotton, lucerne [alfalfa], and pasture, worked by people of a Jewish village, which is raising its children to be honest men and heroes."

She goes on to voice her sympathy for the mothers of the Syrian and Egyptian dead, but concludes: "Better that their mothers should weep than that we should."

Describing a condolence visit, she writes: "We were five sad, strong women sitting there . . . I hope that we will succeed in transmitting a double measure of strength to our young fellow women and our daughters."

It was a brave and moving document and through it all ran not so much a willingness to make sacrifices as an acceptance of the situation because there was no alternative.

During the Lebanon war, too, there were letters redolent with patriotism. One described a visit to a father who had lost his son and said, "It is forbidden to weep for someone who fell in the defense of his people, for his blood was not shed in vain." He did not know of any war more justified than Israel's strike against the terrorists, the father continued. "I went to console," concluded the letter, "and was myself consoled."

However, in this war, for the first time, there were letters of a different type. Painful, angry letters from bereaved parents stated baldly that their sons had died in vain, that they had been "murdered" in an unnecessary war.

Nehama Agmon, a consultant with a Jerusalem mental health center, told the Reuters news agency, "This war, which was launched by Israel, ultimately may not be seen by the public as a heroic chapter. The bereaved may be left with a desolate feeling of having lost a loved one for nothing. In the long run, the ability of families to cope with their grief may depend on whether or not the Israelis feel the war and its toll were justified."

Her remarkably clear-sighted comment was made in the first month of the war and its accuracy was soon evident, as the bitter letters flowed in to the editorial offices. Some of the bitterest reactions came from the parents of six young soldiers who were killed in the battle for Beaufort Castle in South Lebanon.

Beaufort Castle is a Crusader ruin set atop a towering hill over the river Litani, dominating a whole string of Christian and Shiite villages. Well dug in, the PLO would shell the villages from their massive rock dugout, which seemed impervious even to IDF bombing raids. Beaufort Castle had become a symbol of menace for the South Lebanon villages.

On the first night of the war, the elite Golani reconnaissance unit climbed the steep slopes and stormed the almost impregnable fortress. They did not complete its capture until the following morning, and six of their finest soldiers, including their commander, Major Guni Harnik, were killed.

Harnik should not have been there at all. He had completed his conscript army service and followed it by several terms of regular army service. Finally discharged, he had just started to return his military equipment when the war broke out. He at once rushed to join his old unit and took over the command after the field commander was wounded.

"The minute Guni got to the Beaufort and the boys heard his voice, it gave them a sense of security," Eran, one of his soldiers, told the army radio later. "We all felt that things were in the hands of someone who knew what he was doing." Shalom, another soldier, added, "The capture of the Beaufort was Guni's, there are no two ways about it. I just don't want to think of what would have happened after the CO was hit, without Guni. It was a mess, but the minute Guni came, everything tightened up. We knew that there was someone to follow and we followed him. Guni saved the situation."

Guni Harnik's mother, Raya, told the local Jerusalem weekly, *Kol Ha'ir*, (Voice of the Town): "I knew that when Begin yelled his threats at election meetings, it would be Guni and his comrades who would have to pay the debt. Guni felt that the destiny of Israel was on his shoulders."

Raya Harnik, as a widow, could have demanded that her son not serve in a front-line unit, but she knew that she could not prevent her idealistic son from volunteering. The left-wing youth movements provided most of the best combat troops, she said.

She recalled how Guni had talked about leaving the army after the re-election of the Begin government. "Let the heroes of Gush Emunim run up and down the hills," he had commented. But in the end he had signed on for another stretch. "You don't really think we can leave the defense of Israel to them, do you?" he had asked his mother.

Since her husband's death, Guni had been not only a son, but Raya's best friend. She poured out her heart in an interview with a woman's magazine. "Guni is dead and I feel guilty because of the patriotic education I gave him. I spilled his blood. He wasn't killed in a war for our country but in a cynical, political war."

Among Guni's best officers and best friends was Yaron Zamir from En Dor, a kibbutz in Lower Galilee, who died with the young major on the slopes leading to Beaufort Castle. Yehoshua Zamir, his father, wrote to several papers, enclosing a copy of the letter he had written to Ariel Sharon in reply to the formal condolence letter he received from the defense minister: "We have no intention of letting you participate in our mourning. How can we accept condolences from the initiator of the war in which our son was killed?

"Yaron was not 'taken from us.' He was killed in a useless and unjustified war on foreign soil. Yaron did not give his life for his country; rather, you and your colleagues have turned Israel into an altar on which we sacrifice our young men.

"Yaron was slaughtered in a war which has brought peace neither to Galilee, nor to Israel, nor to Lebanon."

In March 1983, nearly ten months after his son had fallen in the battle for Beaufort Castle, I went to see Yehoshua Zamir and his wife, Rama, at their beautiful kibbutz, which nestles, green and fertile, under the looming, bulbous shape of Mount Tabor, where Deborah and Barak had assembled the tribes of ancient Israel to fight the chariots of Sisera.

It was a bright spring day after a long, rainy winter, and the sun was shining for the first time in many weeks, but there was no sun shining in the Zamirs' living room, where the air was still heavy with grief and pain.

Yaron's picture hit me straight between the eyes the minute I walked in the door. He was one of those beautiful sabra kids who shine with a sort of luminosity. I was to learn a great deal about Yaron Zamir, but it was really all there in the portrait. Yehoshua, a photographer of genius, had caught everything of his son's glowing vitality in the instant his shutter clicked, and preserved it forever.

Yehoshua and Rama Zamir were both born in the United States sixty-two years ago — he in Rochester, New York, she in Chicago. After spending much of his youth in Palestine, Yehoshua immigrated "illegally" in 1945. Rama came the following year and they joined a settlement group of the left-wing Hashomer Hatzair youth movement, which settled in En Dor in 1947, a year before the establishment of the new state.

For the next three decades Yehoshua, Rama, and their comrades devoted their lives to building their commune, a society in which none have incomes or private property beyond their few personal possessions, where each labors according to his means, and each receives according to his needs.

They succeeded to a large extent in living on good terms with their Arab neighbors in the villages of Dabburiya, Kafr Masra, and Arab es-Shibli. Yehoshua employed his photographic talents in the cause of coexistence. In a letter written to console his friend for the loss of a son in the Yom Kippur War, he wrote: "I intend to continue my work in the Arab village next door, and today I am clear, more than ever before, about what I want to say in this album . . . I want to state as clearly as black and white can say: Arab and Jew can live together on this piece of land. The more we get to know and understand about our neighbors, the greater the chances for coexistence and peace."

Rama worked as a children's nurse in the communal nursery. Yehoshua was a farmer for many years and then became headmaster of the kibbutz high school. The couple have three children older than Yaron: Tamar lives at En Dor with her husband and baby, Gilad and his family live at a kibbutz nearby, and Naomi teaches at the Bezalel Art College in Jerusalem.

Yehoshua is tall, white-haired, bespectacled; his wife, slim, sensitive, gracefully aging. They are the very personification of the intellectual peasant, the quintessential kibbutznik couple.

Life is often cruel and random, sometimes plucking away the best and brightest without favoritism, but in war in Israel it is worse than that, for fate is weighted negatively against our finest sons: those who volunteer for the elite IDF units. Yaron was such a boy. His parents find themselves unable to console themselves with the argument that he died so that others might live, because they do not believe this to be so. They cannot say it was by chance or fate, because it was not.

"It is bad enough that they took our son from us," said Yehoshua, "but when they try to take away from us the sort of country we wanted Israel to be . . ." He could not complete the sentence. The strong farmer broke down, his face crumpled in agony and he wept.

"It's all right, it's all right." He brushed aside his wife's consolation. "He knows quite well he didn't come to see me for a good cup of coffee and a simple chat."

We walked to the kibbutz cemetery, where no fewer than twelve of the sons of En Dor, victims in the country's wars since 1948, lay buried. Idealistic, socialist En Dor, dedicated to coexistence with its Arab neighbors, has paid a heavy price for its utopia.

The sun was a red ball of fire, sinking behind Mount Tabor, as we stood by Yaron's grave. "I can't get it out of my mind that Yaron was what we made him," said Yehoshua. Yaron, who had problems with his back, should never have been in the crack reconnaissance unit. Turned down by a number of the elite units, he had joined the regular Golani brigade and worked his way into the special unit by sheer guts and persistence. Yehoshua was repeating the sentiments of Raya Harnik: "I made him what he was: I killed him."

I knew how he felt. My own son had volunteered for a top combat unit. We try to educate them to be humane and loving, so that they are not thirsty for conflict, and at the same time to be brave and responsible, so they will not shirk the battle. They are, to some extent, what we make them, but at a certain point their own individuality takes over and they make their own decisions. They are remarkably clear-thinking — even tough-minded. We did indeed thrust them into this dilemma that is Israel, but they would not have had it otherwise. It is easier for me to think this way than it is for Yehoshua, who has lost that which is most dear to him and feels responsible for it.

The parents of the six who died on the Beaufort got together and demanded an explanation from the army for the death of their sons. Even the one couple of them who supported the concept of the war could not understand the Beaufort battle. After some prevarication, the IDF sent a senior commander to talk to them, but they were not convinced. They are sure the castle should not have been taken as it was: not at night and not without armored corps support.

Back in his room, Yehoshua showed me a letter in which he had written Prime Minister Begin, "We live here in the Lower Galilee at peace with our Arab neighbors, and in this spirit I raised my children. Yet what could I say to the [Arab] neighbor who came to console me at the death of my son Yaron, on the very day that members of his own family were being bombarded in the city of Sidon?"

He described his anguish at the prime minister's televised appearance on Beaufort Castle, in which he commented on the purity of the air and was told by the defense minister that the position had been taken "without IDF casualties."

"You cannot bring my son back to me," he wrote, "but you can desist from further bereavement and agony. Cease the shelling of civilians in Lebanon!"

And Begin wrote back: "There never was a more just campaign

in our country, or anywhere else, than the campaign which was given the justified name 'Operation Peace for Galilee'; the name of your son, Yaron, will be for ever inscribed in the annals of the nation."

Yehoshua had thrown himself into demonstrations against the war. He had been with Shuki and his friends on the night that their protest vigil outside the prime minister's office was attacked. "After they had gone," he told me, "we stood and wept because of the lack of communication between us. We could not reach them and they would not speak to us."

Many, however, did hear about the Zamirs and communicated with them. A fifteen-year-old girl wrote: "I was deeply moved that at such a difficult time you are prepared to express your views publicly, to participate in the activities of Soldiers against Silence, and work for an end to the war."

When Eli Geva resigned, Zamir phoned him to express his admiration and the young colonel came to En Dor to console Yehoshua. Many others came or wrote.

An American friend, Professor George Stoney of New York, wrote: "You are mourning not just the loss of a son, but the loss of an ideal for which you have given your life."

When I left En Dor, I took with me the collection of diaries, letters, and poems that Yehoshua had found in his son's room. It also included letters written by Yaron that his many friends had sent, on his son's death, for Yehoshua to copy. For the next two days I immersed myself in the documents, watching Yaron grow from a precocious child into a brash teen-ager and then into a sensitive young man.

Yaron grew up in a time of wars. He was seven at the time of the Six Day War, thirteen in the Yom Kippur War, and eighteen in Operation Litani. One of the first things he ever wrote, at the age of seven, was a poem, which included the lines:

> If I had a magician's hat,
> I would ask for peace . . .

A year later, he writes to the leader of Egypt: "Nasser, we want peace . . ."

And, aged thirteen:

> To the memory of our soldiers, who fell standing guard,
> A shame for every one of them.
> I was small and did not know them all,
> But I know they did not die for nothing.

Growing up, Yaron conducts a delightful teen-age flirtation with Hannah, from another kibbutz: "It is important for me to know what you think of me . . . I hope you have remained as beautiful as you used to be."

She replies disingenuously: "I am not too tall or too short; too fat or too thin; too clever or too stupid — I am very average. I like to read poetry."

"We had something between us," he replies, "don't deny it."

He writes to his other friends about sports, particularly basketball, which he loved. Yehoshua writes to his daughter: "At last I have found a common language with my young son. He is training me to be a basketball player, and I almost kill myself with that pace-and-a-half . . . I have promised to start reading the sports pages."

On Yehoshua's birthday, Yaron writes him a poem:

> To my father, who has remained a joker,
> And who always helps out — even in a crisis,
> To Abba [Dad], the photographer,
> From your loving son, who loves you so much.

Grown up and about to go into the army, he writes in the class journal:

> Do you know my name?
> I am called Yaron.
> Everyone thinks that I am just crazy,
> But they don't understand how

It is wonderful to be free and to make fun of
Serious things, and to laugh at the whole world.

On a serious note, he writes to Dalit: "You are becoming a
woman, which is a wonderful stage in your life." From the army
he writes home, always starting with a cheerful "Hello parents,"
and going on to share his thoughts and experiences with them.
"When you return to the base, you sometimes go into a depression
that you don't think will ever lift, but it goes and the smiles come
out again . . . "

He writes to Idit: "I am a bit disappointed that, at the age of
twenty, I still have not had a serious girlfriend. I cannot get away
from this habit of looking into the future."

He feels affection for both Dalit and Idit. To Idit, he writes: "I
am going to sleep and I hope I'll dream of you." And to Dalit:
"How lovely it was to be with you." Then again to Idit: "My Idit,
I now know that we are together . . . It is love again."

But then, tragedy strikes: Yaniv, a lifelong friend, dies of a
heart attack, during military training. Yaron eulogizes him, recalling their friendship and their basketball, with which it was
inextricably intertwined. He writes to Yaniv's girl, Yael: "Remember, there is someone who thinks of you, who worries, who
cares, even if Yaniv is no more."

He writes to Idit: "After Yaniv's death, I entered a black period,
a time of apathy and emptiness. It is difficult for me to enjoy the
things I once enjoyed."

A few months later he writes to Yael: "I so much want to come
to you and hug you and do the things that Yaniv now cannot
do . . . I feel so inadequate."

Yael replies: "You know how to surprise, a surprise that struck
me like a warm wave, creating light. You know how to arrive at
the crucial moment and to bring help . . . I am so grateful for
what you are to me. You are simply good — good-hearted — thank
you."

"I want to cry," he confides to her. "It is a shame that I do not have your shoulder to cry on." And she writes back: "I do not want there to be harmony with his perpetual absence."

In his letters Yaron pours out his feelings on a wide range of subjects, and we find him increasingly worried about the political situation. To Yael he writes: "I know things that many in the army and ordinary civilians do not know. It is a strange feeling, a sort of pressure in the stomach. I can't go into more detail." And only three months before the war, he writes to Dalit: "I am very worried about the possibility of war . . . I don't pretend to be a prophet, but the current situation is very depressing."

And finally, this letter, which could serve as his epitaph, written to Yona, another girlfriend, two weeks before his death: "To speak openly without lying, to be honest even if it hurts, to tell each other the truth to our faces. I very much believe in this honest approach. I am sure that you have plenty to tell me . . . We just have to find the right time and place."

Many of Yaron's poems and letters have been published in a memorial booklet, which Yehoshua prepared for his son. He wanted to make it a "cry of pain," but his family persuaded him that this would not do justice to the sort of person that Yaron was. He spent hours with his son's letters and jottings, "as if I can perform a miracle and resurrect him thus. At least I can re-create the moments in which he wrote them."

Speaking at Yaron's grave, a year after his son's death, Yehoshua quoted the words written by Yaron, with which he ends the booklet:

> To remember the past,
> To live the present,
> To trust the future.

"It is difficult to trust the future," said Yehoshua, "when your future is laid dead before you. But to remain faithful to the spirit of Yaron's words, we have gathered here today to try and search for the path ahead, not to be discouraged, not to give up."

Explaining why he had continued throughout the year to cry

out with his pain and to condemn the war, he appealed again for
an end to the conflict and called on the government to bring the
soldiers home. He could not save Yaron, he knew that, but at
least the death of others could be prevented.

"We are not consoled," he declared, "and we can never be
consoled, because Yaron should not have been killed."

Yehoshua's one-man campaign of letter writing, demonstrating,
and lobbying has not been tied to any one movement of the many
that have sprung up in the wake of this war, but he has naturally
felt a particular closeness to one called Parents against Silence.

This movement, in the words of a founder, "to parallel the
Soldiers against Silence movement established by our wonderful
sons," has become one of the most eloquent voices against the
war, lobbying, writing, demonstrating, holding vigils outside Prime
Minister Begin's home in Jerusalem. Its leaders were received
by both Begin and the new defense minister, Moshe Arens. Many
Israelis who were never before active in public affairs have joined
their ranks.

At a recent demonstration outside the Knesset, one of the or-
ganizers read the following poem by "an anonymous mother":

> Being the mother of a soldier in Lebanon,
> Is to tremble each time you hear the helicopter's roar,
> And to jump each time the phone rings,
> And to freeze with shock at each knock on the door.
> Our boys do not complain: only their eyes speak . . .
> Their bodies are now tired, and they have strength,
> But in their hearts there are questions and their souls know
>   no rest.
> Forgive us, our sons, that, this once,
> We presume to break our silence and shout aloud.

Not all the "boys" have kept silent. Many of them have demonstrated and there is a growing movement of young men who

refuse to serve in Lebanon — an entirely new phenomenon in Israel. There was always the conscientious objector, or two, and a handful who refused to serve in the occupied territories, but it was never as wide-scale as it is today.

Yesh Gvul, "There's a limit," is still a minority movement. Peace Now does not support refusal of service, and Eli Geva, the most famous dissident, has spoken out strongly against it, but more than sixty soldiers have been sentenced for refusing to serve and the movement claims that over two thousand have signed its petition, including two hundred and ninety reserve officers.

At a Jerusalem press conference, three youngsters from the new movement claimed that whereas their members report to their units and then ask openly to serve somewhere else than Lebanon, many others try to evade service by other methods. This is certainly borne out by what I have heard from the young soldiers of my son's generation, who describe crowds of more than a hundred waiting for "personal discussions" with their battalion commanders. One young soldier told me he had written to his brother, who was traveling abroad, advising him not to hurry back — a complete reversal of the Israeli tradition that in times of crisis, it is the "done thing" to hurry home and report to your unit.

Another reservist told me that when he got to his unit, the CO said straight out, "Okay, those who want to refuse should know that they'll get thirty-five days' jail, followed by thirty-five days' folding blankets in the store of a camp — and then you are out of the unit."

The youngsters take considerable pride in serving in their special units. They have volunteered and undergone years of incredibly tough training. They know and respect their fellows, both as friends and as fighters. They have absolute trust in one another and want to be together in battle, if it comes. It is difficult enough to get into one of these units; it is more difficult to stand the course and yet more difficult to decide to give it all up. Understandably, the young soldiers are reluctant to take the ultimate step, for if a defensive war breaks out, they want to play their part and they want to do so with their comrades.

At the Yesh Gvul news conference, one Dudu Palma explained how he had summoned up the determination to make the break. A thick-set, broad-shouldered kibbutznik from Kefar Hanassi in Galilee, with bright blue eyes under a high forehead, wearing T-shirt and jeans, he spoke in a laconic, clipped sabra style of speech that was remarkably effective.

"When I volunteered for an elite IDF unit, I thought I would be fighting to defend my country," he said. "Suddenly I found myself fighting on land that was not mine. There was a value that I took seriously: fighting for our existence. This value has been destroyed.

"This was a year in which many concepts were destroyed. First they destroyed the concept of ain brera, then they destroyed the concept of the emergency mobilization order. I always knew that when that type of order came, I had to close my eyes and go out to battle. Today the only emergency mobilization order that I recognize is the one in my heart."

Dudu and eighteen comrades found themselves in a military jail, along with boys who had hit their CO, smuggled goods from Lebanon, or stolen vehicles. "They did not really know what to do with us in jail," he told us. "But we were treated okay."

Dudu Palma is one of a group of young soldiers from his kibbutz who grew up fast in 1982. Their stenciled magazine, Kol Soteh ("Every Nonconformist"), was similar to all the journals dealing with gossip, farming news, sports, and social events that are produced by kibbutz children, but under the impact of the war, Kol Soteh turned into a sharp, bitter "underground" tract. Its articles found their way into the general magazines of the kibbutz movement and thence into the national press.

Kefar Hanassi is a particularly successful commune with a vibrant social and cultural life. Many of its members were born in England and are known to me personally. It was established during the 1948 War of Independence, and its members strug-

gled for years with both the unfamiliar soil of their rocky environment and the unfamiliar customs of their new land. Eventually
its factory, which makes irrigation equipment, flourished, its agriculture prospered, and today it is one of the country's finest
settlements.

The adults are still very "English," down to the accent of their
Hebrew, but their children are sabras. *Kol Soteh*, with its harsh,
brash tone, has caused more than raised eyebrows among the
older generation. One of the covers (showing a nude creature,
with an enormous male organ, bearing the prime minister's head
on a platter) was banned, leading to a lively public meeting at
which the matter was thrashed out.

"I was personally offended by that cover," exclaimed one of
the veterans, but other parents were more tolerant. Many lauded
the existence of *Kol Soteh*; however, one remarked, almost wist-
fully, "It is a question of language. The youngsters and the veterans understand certain words in different ways."

The journal's editor, Ronen, put it rather more pithily: "It might
as well be written in Chinese. Our parents just don't understand
how we feel."

In an article describing the attack on the En Hilwe refugee
camp, Dudu Palma, who was later to refuse to serve in Lebanon,
wrote: "The meaning of *hilwe* in Arabic is 'sweet.' The smell of
dead corpses is also sweet, mingled with the sweet smell of the
orange groves." And he continued, "For us, the nasty work started
when we watched the interrogators sorting out the terrorists from
the civilians. You try to convince yourself that this is a necessary
step in the war against terror. That you are a big boy now, that
it's time you grew up.

"But I, who cry when I watch 'Little House on the Prairie' on
television, could not bear to watch those interrogators working."

Dudu catches a lift home with a German journalist, "who thinks
we are something special," and who asks him what it was like
in En Hilwe. "Like the Warsaw ghetto," Dudu tells him, "and I
watch the smile on his face turn cold."

Ronen castigates the older generation who criticize *Kol Soteh*:

"So the youth of today are not what they were . . . they drink beer to blur the senses from the chaos you bequeathed them. Once youth drained the swamps; now they drain their beer glasses."

Avishai writes to the older member who had been offended by the obscene cover: "I understand your disgust: it is a bit frightening, a bit disgusting, a bit provocative, but I am frightened, disgusted, and provoked by what Begin is preparing for us."

A contributor writes to Imri, the son of Defense Minister Sharon: "I was glad to discover that Sharon had a son in the army. I hope you will ask him what he is doing, what we are doing in Lebanon. I hope you will cause his heart to contract, so that this father will learn what other fathers knew a long time ago."

Etai writes to the chief of staff: "Don't talk to me about our strength and about how ready we are for the next war. I want to know how to *prevent* the next war!"

Talking to a group of the young people who write and produce *Kol Soteh*, I find them, for the first time, pouring out their innermost thoughts to me. They are the children of my lifelong friends, but hitherto we have only exchanged courtesies. The transformation of their journal was not planned, says assistant editor Sarah, but the war released "a torrent of words that could not be dammed." Petite and pretty, Sarah frowns as she admits that it is entirely a boys' show. She is on the sidelines.

"It worries me a lot," she admits. "But what can I do? This is the Israeli reality: it is the boys who have to go to war, the boys who see what is happening, the boys who raise the shout of anger."

Oran is big and brown and strong, with the craggy face and husky voice of his father, but without his father's conventional views. He serves, like so many of them, in one of the special units.

"We argued from the very first day," he declares, noting that his was the unit that sent a critical letter to the prime minister in the early weeks of the war. "We had a hell of a lot of questions and received very few answers from our superior officers."

He went on to talk about the West Bank. "It hurts me more than Lebanon even. I used to think that we were the 'good guys' in the Israel-Arab argument and that the others didn't want to understand us. In the West Bank we are the 'bad guys' and we are very bad. I can understand how the young West Bank Arab grows up to be a terrorist."

For all his criticisms, Oran would not live anywhere else. He did not decide this on the basis of ideology; his love of the land is very physical. "I love the countryside, the mountains — even the people. I hate military service — every day of it — but I love the IDF; I am addicted to it. I can't do without it.

"I don't like the Israeli from Tel Aviv or Rosh Pina, but I am used to him. I can't live without the Israeli mentality or the Israeli food. I have traveled in the world and I know there are more beautiful places, richer places, better places, but I only feel at home here. I love this stinking country!"

His girlfriend (shortly afterward to be his wife), Tamar, added, "In Europe it is so wonderful that there are borders without fences and barbed wire, but we will see it too, even if it takes until I am sixty. There will be peace between us and our neighbors. I believe it with all my heart."

"We are at a crossroad," cuts in Ronen. "Something pretty drastic is going to happen in this country, but people have started communicating, talking to each other. I get around, I talk to people. Things are stirring, even among the Edot. There are arguments and arguments can lead to violence, but at least we are beginning to communicate."

Oran caps this statement by saying that the war has strengthened his conviction that Israel must do the unthinkable — talk to the PLO. Israel has to share the land with the Palestinians.

I remind him gently that Kefar Hanassi was established on land that formerly belonged to Arabs.

"That was before I was born," he snapped. "I am not responsible for what happened then. I am responsible for what is happening today."

I was enormously impressed with his response. We spend so much time in mulling over the past, wallowing in Jewish persecution over the ages, refighting the battles of 1948, 1967, and 1973, arguing the historic rights and wrongs, the justices, and the injustices. Oran's pragmatism, cutting through the bullshit, gets right to the heart of the matter. It is wonderfully sabra and wonderfully refreshing. It refuses to take refuge in history and forces us to look ahead. It holds out hope for the future.

Oran, Dudu, Ronen, and the others were youngsters, caught up in their first war, but for my friend, Rami — like me, in his late forties — it was also his first experience of battle. Like all of us, he had been called up for past wars, but had never before gotten to the front line.

Rami's war diary, scribbled almost illegibly on grubby bits of paper, is a remarkably immediate document. There had been no time for reflection or rationalization.

After his baptism of fire in the school yard of the Rashadiye refugee camp, when a shell almost falls on top of him, Rami proceeds to Tyre, finding it, with its natural bay and delicate minarets, beautiful, but then, "as we draw near, the beauty changes to an understanding of what Tyre really looks like, feels like, smells like. The picture of beauty takes a little while to pass. Slowly the reality strikes home. It's not possible that we did such devastation! No shop not blasted, buildings crumpled under their roofs, boats sunk in the bay . . . and above all the overwhelming stench that we met before around the rotting bodies in the village."

Like Dudu, he is revolted by the treatment of terrorist suspects, who are slapped around and beaten by the interrogators. He accepts the necessity of uncovering information that might safeguard their lives, "But why the joy and laughing by some of the soldiers, standing by watching?"

He approves the blowing up of houses in the refugee camps. "I feel that a place like Rashadiye is so bad that only a total expurgation can restore normalcy . . . We should rehabilitate the inhabitants in a positive atmosphere that won't allow them to be used as pawns in a power game."

A few days later, we read Rami's description of the evacuation of terrorist suspects from a village: "The whole population violently protesting, clinging to the bus, hanging onto the armored half-tracks, rending clothes, screaming, crying. The agony of these poor people is heartbreaking. How can one remain indifferent to the real anguish of a woman who has had her husband or father taken away?

"Can it be that some of the boys are without feelings? I hear them saying that the women need a good kick in the pants."

Rami describes his company commander as "excellent" when he speaks to the troops about how to treat women and children. Despite the talk about "kick in the pants," the soldiers behave well toward the women and the children, but they are less scrupulous when it comes to the male population.

An IDF company commander is missing (his body, thrown into a well, will be found later). Rami accepts the need for tough interrogations, but he is disgusted when he sees a young soldier "joining in with glee. I really got mad with him and hope I made him see how wrong he was. Unfortunately, Jews are no different from other people. Quite a few are heartless and cruel and use the opportunity to act out feelings of superiority on poor, helpless prisoners."

One of the strongest critics of the war was Lieutenant Colonel Dov Irmiya, at sixty-nine the oldest senior officer in active service. A veteran combat officer, he was nevertheless disgusted at the lack of humanity shown by many IDF soldiers and is certain that it represents a sharp deterioration from the standards set in previous wars.

"If I had wanted to chronicle the good deeds of IDF troops in Lebanon, I could have filled three volumes," he told me. "Of course, many of the soldiers — particularly from the combat units — behaved decently. They gave water to prisoners from their own bottles, tended the wounded at risk to their own safety, gave sweets to the children, calmed the frightened women. But I am not interested in whether we are better than the Syrians, or the PLO, or the Lebanese themselves. We have to be perfect!"

I first met Irmiya in the ruins of the En Hilwe refugee camp in the winter after the war. He had been dismissed from the army after publicly criticizing the war and the behavior of many of the IDF soldiers in Lebanon. Supported by funds from a committee of Galilee Jews and Arabs, he was running a private refugee aid project, which he had established.

The camp had been almost completely destroyed. The road was potholed and muddy, the sewage flowed in the streets. Rusting bed frames, abandoned vehicles, cans, bottles, plastic bags, cartons, and orange peel were strewn around.

Here and there refugee families, largely without their males, who had been imprisoned by the IDF at the Ansar detention camp, were rebuilding their homes with cement provided by the American Joint Distribution Committee and Irmiya's committee. Irmiya was discussing his project with Dr. Fikri, a Palestinian doctor who at that time headed a local residents' committee in the camp.

Irmiya is the very personification of the old-style pioneer. Thick gray hair and mustache frame a deeply lined brown face, which looks as if it was carved in mahogany. He speaks with the fervor of an ancient Hebrew prophet and the conviction of a left-wing Zionist ideologue.

His career spans the struggle for Jewish statehood. He served in the Haganah defense organization in the 1930s, volunteered for the British army in World War II, smuggled "illegal" Jewish immigrants into Palestine, served as a company commander and deputy battalion commander in the IDF, taught Hebrew to newcomers in the 1950s, and joined a kibbutz.

After his service in the regular army, Irmiya was active in civil defense in the north of Israel, and in 1974 he was cited for his part in the battle with a terrorist gang, which took hostages in the northern coastal town of Nahariya.

As a reserve officer he served in the IDF aid unit for South Lebanon both in the Litani operation and the recent war. After a number of media interviews, in which he criticized the behavior of some IDF troops and specifically his own aid unit, he published *My War Diary*, an account of his experiences during the Lebanon war.

The diary does not tell a pretty story. Irmiya asserts that the claim of tohar haneshek was in many cases phony. He records numerous examples of brutality and insensitivity on the part of some soldiers and certain units. Challenged that he was giving ammunition to Israel's enemies, he responded, "It is our actions that harm Israel — not what people write about those actions."

He asserts that in the first days of the war, after the conquest of Tyre and Sidon, curfews, arrests, and harassment of the local population were out of all proportion to the danger of terrorist attacks on IDF troops. His own aid unit actually hindered efforts by the locals to help themselves. Although they were under orders to extend assistance to the local population, many officers in the aid unit showed a notable lack of sympathy with its plight.

When Ya'acov Meridor, the Israeli cabinet minister in charge of the aid program, visited Sidon he was given an upbeat briefing by a local aid officer and told (untruthfully) that the locals were sabotaging the aid effort to make Israel look bad.

Asked what should be done with the refugees, Meridor gestured toward the north with his hands and said, "Push them out and don't let them come back." This attitude from the top, he maintains, led to a combination of brutality and apathy.

In the book's most striking passage, he describes the prolonged detention of some six hundred local citizens in a monastery yard in Sidon. The prisoners sat in rows in the sun, hands tied behind their backs, hungry, thirsty, frightened, and, in some cases, wounded. IDF soldiers passed down the rows, beating them with clubs and pulling them into line by their hair.

One prisoner sat propped against a pillar while an IDF officer repeatedly kicked him in his already bleeding face. When Irmiya remonstrated, he was told, "This one is dangerous. He has been trying to loosen his bonds. I am making an example of him. We don't want them sticking knives in our backs!"

Later, this same officer came to Irmiya and said plaintively, "We were told to be tough with them; now you come along and tell me off. Why don't you make up your minds?"

I told Irmiya that I thought he had painted an exaggeratedly negative picture of the situation. As a veteran of service in Gaza, I thought I knew a subdued population when I saw one, I said, and I had found the Lebanese cheerful and unafraid.

"Look here," he said, "I did not say we were going through the streets murdering and pillaging. Of course the Lebanese — and the Palestinians — were impressed with the IDF's behavior, but it isn't good enough to be better than the others. Furthermore, eight people did die in captivity in those first three days in Sidon. I don't know whether there was an investigation, but no one has been made to answer for it. To me this is a catastrophe."

I challenged his story about Meridor's remarks. The refugees had not been expelled, I noted. He was unimpressed. It was more a lack of efficiency and planning, he thought. For example, the families of the young men in the Ansar detention camp had refused to leave. The whole matter had simply not been thought out.

Irmiya insisted that there had been a decline in standards and that the decline was from the top. In the Litani Operation, Ezer Weizman had been defense minister and the relief effort had been superb. There were admittedly fewer problems then, because there had been a genuine desire to help. In this war, there was little desire to help. He had personally been reprimanded for endangering himself by traveling among the population alone and at night.

"I told my CO that if we can take risks to kill, we can take risks to bring aid and comfort," he told me proudly.

Irmiya insists that there has been a steady decline in the IDF. The degeneration started a long time ago, he maintains, as soon as the volunteer Haganah turned into a professional army.

"I am a purist," he admits. "For me the ideal army was the

Haganah — and particularly the Palmach. The Palmach kib-butznik was a farmer, but as soon as the IDF came along you had officers in posh cars, and it was the beginning of the end."

Israel lives on its might, and rightly so, says Irmiya. There is no alternative, although a country that lives on might must even-tually become corrupt. "Even justified might is corrupting," he insists.

In his diary Irmiya wrote of his disgust at the religious soldiers who sang fervent Sabbath songs on the first Friday night of the war. "I hate them," he wrote. "I am ashamed to belong to a people which sings over dead bodies."

I challenged him on this passage, but he would not retract. "They were singing to celebrate victory and the Sabbath," he maintains. "All I could think about was the smell of rotting corpses."

As an atheist he is depressed about the revival of religion, as represented by Gush Emunim, in the country. The traditional Jewish hatred of the goy, the justifiable result of persecution, is being perverted into a hatred of the Arab, a hatred not unlike that of the Gentile for the Jew.

Zionism succeeded as long as it was moral, he believes. If it is becoming immoral, it is doomed. A new "Arab Zionism," based on Zion (Jerusalem), might prevail. The Jewish people was de-stroyed two thousand years ago by the zealots who fought Rome, "and today the zealots are running things again."

Irmiya is deeply pessimistic about Israeli society, but "the one thing that I haven't given up on is my right to struggle." He throws himself into his work for the relief committee, often vis-iting the Palestinian camps in South Lebanon. During the war, he says, he fought to get another water tanker and more food and clothing to the prisoners. After the active phase of the war he was collecting money and fighting the bureaucrats to get prefabricated classrooms to En Hilwe and the other camps.

Dov Irmiya is truly hewn in the prophetic mold, but thousands of ordinary Israelis are also finding their voices and protesting. In the early days of the war the protesters were in a minority.

Numerically they probably still are, but the protest grew. The daily attrition made even government supporters weary of the conflict, but the turning point, the events that shook the foundations of the new Israel — the Israel of Menachem Begin — were the massacres in Sabra and Shatila.

Fewer than a thousand people were killed, a smaller number than in the bombing and shelling. Furthermore, the massacres were carried out by Christian Phalangist forces, but the events in the Beirut camps awoke ancient echoes, reverberating down the corridors of Jewish history.

On September 1, when the last of the Syrians and the PLO left Beirut, things looked good for Begin and Sharon. Bashir Jemayel was president of Lebanon, the PLO had been routed, the Syrians humiliated.

Two weeks later the "new order" lay in ruins. Bashir Jemayel and several dozen of his Phalangist officers had been killed in an enormous explosion. I remember buying a paper with the screaming headlines. Jerusalem was buzzing; there was no other topic of conversation.

Later, Eli Geva was to say to me with bitter sarcasm, "Of course they were surprised. After all, no one has ever before been assassinated in the Arab world — not the leaders of Syria and Iraq, not Saudi King Faisal, not President Sadat!"

Immediately after Bashir's assassination was verified Begin and Sharon decided to send the IDF into West Beirut, "to prevent the danger of violence, bloodshed, and anarchy," in the words of the subsequent cabinet statement. But the IDF did not go into the Palestinian camps. This job was given to the Christian Phalangists, who, in some forty hours, massacred about seven hundred civilians, including women and children.

The reawakened echoes were not those of the Nazi Holocaust, but of the Russian pogroms. Around the world so much has been written, comparing Sabra and Shatila to the Holocaust, that the time has come to put the matter in perspective.

The Nazi Holocaust of the Jews of Europe was unprovoked murder of unarmed civilians on a scale unparalleled in human history. In his *Atlas of the Holocaust*, historian Martin Gilbert drew a map showing the places seventeen representative victims came from and described each of them in a couple of sentences. He then noted: "If a similarly short reference was made to each Jew murdered between 1939 and 1945, 353,000 such maps would be needed. To draw these maps at the author's and cartographer's fastest rate of a map a day would take more than 967 years."

One can also observe differences between the Beirut massacres and a pogrom. When the IDF went into West Beirut it was attacked: fire was directed on its troops from Shatila, and the Phalangists also suffered a few casualties when they entered the camps. But a description of the most famous Russian pogrom — that in Kishinev in 1903 — will suffice to show disturbing similarities.

The Kishinev pogrom began on the first day of Passover, when an anti-Jewish mob ran riot in the town's Jewish neighborhood. Agents of the Ministry of the Interior were reportedly arousing the mob, and the czarist army garrison refused to intervene. The rampage lasted for a day and a night, during which forty-nine Jews were killed and five hundred injured. The rioters looted and destroyed some six hundred businesses and seven hundred homes.

The IDF did not incite the Phalangists; on the contrary, Israeli officers repeatedly warned the Phalangist commanders not to harm civilians. However, the image of IDF soldiers failing to intervene, while civilians were being massacred nearby, conjured up dreadful memories and led to immediate protests outside the prime minister's home in Jerusalem.

The Israeli press was almost unanimous in its condemnation. *Ha'aretz* wrote that "the expulsion of the chief of staff and the defense minister from the ranks of the decision-makers is a primary condition for us to be able to look ourselves in the eye and look the world in the eye." *Davar* warned that "every minister who continues to sit around the cabinet table, and does not resign immediately, acts as if he gives his post-factum approval to the slayings." The *Jerusalem Post* called for the resignation of Begin, Sharon, and the chief of staff and the formation of a caretaker government under one of the deputy prime ministers. *Al-Hamishmar* called on the entire government to resign, to "cleanse the people, the nation, and Zionism."

The government met and issued a statement: "No one will preach moral values or respect for human life to us. A blood libel has been perpetrated against the Jewish people." A more inappropriate response would be difficult to devise.

A blood libel, the charge that Jews were killing Gentile children to make their Passover matzo, had led to the Kishinev pogrom. There had been pogroms in the countries of the Middle East as well as Europe. The pogrom was as much a part of the folk memory of the Edot as it was for European Jews. The Zionist idea is as old as Abraham, but modern Zionism is to a great extent the child of the pogrom. Every Israeli schoolchild has learned about the pogroms. This time the prime minister was out of tune with his nation.

What stood out at the early protests over Sabra and Shatila was, for the first time, the significant numbers of skullcapped religious youths. Things were stirring in the hesder yeshivot, hitherto the strongholds of Gush Emunim. Rabbi Yehuda Amital, head of the Har Etzion yeshiva in the West Bank, called the massacres *Hillul Hashem*, "a desecration of God's name." Religious youths, notably from the hesder yeshivot, were prominent among those demanding an official inquiry into the massacres.

I went to see Amital, a benign but hard-hitting rabbi with horn-rimmed glasses and a full gray beard.

"If our presence did not prevent the Phalangists from doing what they did," he told me, "it is the shame and failure of all of us."

We were sitting in his study, which is not so much book-lined as book-crammed. The black tomes of scholarly Jewish works reach the high ceiling and spill over onto the tables and desks.

A former IDF soldier, Amital hit out against the stereotyping of religious Jews as political hawks. If someone was devoted to the Land of Israel concept, it did not mean he was in favor of the war in Lebanon.

He himself believed in retaining the land for the Jewish people, but thought it is perfectly valid to argue that the welfare of the Jewish people demands giving up part of the land. If he were given a choice between more Jews with less land or more land with fewer Jews, he would take the first option, he declared.

There were three pillars to Judaism, he told me: the Torah (law) of Israel, the people of Israel, and the Land of Israel. Gush Emunim had elevated the land above the other two. The Gush had never had an entirely free run in the national religious camp. There had always been a small countermovement called *Oz Veshalom*, "Peace and Strength," but the religious doves were a small minority of intellectuals, mostly from the universities. In the wake of Sabra and Shatila, the hesder yeshivot gave birth to a new religious movement called *Netivot Shalom*, "Paths to Peace," which was pledged to do battle with the Gush on its home ground.

Zvi Lifshitz, knitted skullcap clipped to his blond hair, sat by his computer in his modern computer services office and told me about his new movement. Netivot Shalom was born after the massacres, he told me, but it had been conceived at Yamit.

"I used to be a supporter of Gush Emunim," he admitted. "I thought that in the absence of peace, we ought to go all-out to settle the entire Land of Israel." Then came Sadat and the peace process. When the final phase of the Sinai withdrawal reached its farcical climax and the Gush led the physical resistance to evacuation, "I saw religious Jews leading the battle against peace and I said to myself: they don't represent me."

The new movement quickly took up a position with regard to the West Bank. They pledged their devotion to the Land of Israel, but they noted that there might be a clash between holding on to all the land and peace. Peace, according to Torah morality, must prevail, they argued. They also maintained that depriving a million Arabs of their civil rights could not be reconciled with Torah morality. When the values of land and Torah clash, they declared, it is the Torah which is supreme.

The response to Netivot Shalom surprised its founders. In the words of one of them, "An awful lot of religious doves came out of the closet." For years, Gush Emunim members had been the pacesetters in the religious camp; they would no longer go unchallenged.

The message got through to the members of the National Religious party. Education Minister Zvulon Hammer, one of the founders of Gush Emunim, went on television to say that veneration of the Land of Israel may harm Israel's interests and the spirit of Judaism "if it is not balanced by other fundamental Jewish values." The right of Jews to settle in the Land of Israel did not mean the right to dominate another people, he cautioned.

Hammer and the other ministers of his party were among those who fought hardest inside the cabinet for a proper inquiry into the massacre, an inquiry Begin and Sharon did everything in their power to resist. Another remarkable intervention was that of Yitzhak Navon, the president of Israel.

Never before had a president made such an intervention. The presidency in Israel is a powerless office, a sort of elected constitutional monarchy. Navon was the most popular president Israel ever had. Born in the country, but of parents from Turkey and Morocco, Navon had been an active president, crisscrossing the country from north to south, speaking to the people in their towns and villages in simple, but eloquent language.

He had been scrupulous in avoiding controversial issues, but now he went on television and demanded "a thorough and impartial judicial inquiry" into the massacres. He afterward disclosed that he was prepared to take the unprecedented step of resigning if his demand was not met.

In the IDF, too, there was a ferment. Because of censorship regulations we had to rely on foreign press reports, but it was widely reported that more than a hundred officers of the rank of brigadier and above met with Ariel Sharon and demanded his resignation. The thirty-seven-year-old commander of Israel's crack paratroops reportedly told the minister that after the massacres and the government's reaction to them, he could no longer lead his men "with a clear conscience." When several top officers offered their resignation, strenuous efforts were made to persuade them to stay on.

The world went to town over Sabra and Shatila, but it was among the Jews, and not only in Israel, that the agony was most acute. I have before me the sermon delivered on Yom Kippur, the Day of Atonement, by Rabbi Barry Friedman, the leader of a prosperous New Jersey congregation. Friedman is one of those Jews who feels a strong affinity with Israel. Early in the war he had visited Beirut, talked to Lebanese and IDF soldiers, and returned to vindicate Israel's conduct. The IDF, he had told his congregants only weeks before, had preserved tohar haneshek.

Now he stood before them and said, "This Yom Kippur we move about in a state of deep anguish. You, my congregation, and I are torn, and for so many of us it is the first real challenge to a thirty-four-year love relationship with the State of Israel."

Comparing the clash of the people of Israel with their prime minister to the Biblical prophet Jeremiah's confrontation with the kings of Israel, Friedman said, "It is the wrestling of the human spirit in Israel and our similar struggle here that directs us to the ancient dictum of our people, 'Justice and only justice shall you pursue.' "

In Israel the demand for an inquiry became overwhelming. As a veteran of the big antinuclear marches in Britain in the 1950s, I am not exactly new to demonstrations, but I have never seen a protest like the one in Tel Aviv on Saturday night, one week after the massacres. The crowd has been estimated as four hundred thousand people, more than a tenth of Israel's Jewish population.

Men and women, young and old, soldier and civilian, religious and secular, they flowed into Tel Aviv's main square in a never-ending stream and overflowed into the streets beyond. Elderly pioneers, resting on canes, rubbed shoulders with bare-armed young women; pious bearded Jews in skullcaps stood by hirsute young students. Fathers carried children on their shoulders and young couples strolled hand in hand. They had come from the kibbutzim and the development towns, from the farthest reaches of Galilee and the Negev, from army camps and yeshivot. Above all, the young people dominated: thousands upon thousands of curly, close-cropped, long-haired, open-faced youths, the future of our country.

There is a question that has gnawed away at us Jews since the time of the Holocaust: Why did no one do anything? How often have we repeated this agonizing question to ourselves? We know that there were protesters, that many fine human beings did try to save some of our people, but we also know that too many people averted their gaze and too many countries refused to allow Jews to enter.

I think it is the world's silence that haunts us more than anything else about the Holocaust. We are more prepared to accept the fact that a few thousand crazy, evil men perpetrated the deed than we are to accept what we call "the world's silence."

The Beirut massacres evoked atavistic memories — not least among the young. A young friend of my son said that night, "Anyone who does not come to Tel Aviv tonight should stop asking why no one said anything during the Holocaust!" And in this instance I accept the parallel; that night in Tel Aviv was Israel's answer to the world.

It was the catharsis of a people, a thunderous, anguished cry of protest and penance, a ringing affirmation that "this thing was not done in our name!" In two decades of life in Israel I had not experienced a moment like it. I do not remember the speeches and I don't think they were all that important. I do remember one sentence from Amnon Rubinstein, a member of parliament who had been most eloquent in demanding an inquiry: "I am proud to be an Israeli tonight." He spoke for us all.

Five and a half months later, on February 8, 1983, we reporters assembled at Bet Agron, the Journalists' Association building in Jerusalem, to receive our copies of the report of the judicial commission of inquiry into "the events at the refugee camps in Beirut."

In a country where "leaks" are a way of life, where everyone knows everyone else and most journalists are on first-name terms with several cabinet ministers and half the Knesset, the contents of the report were kept an amazingly closely guarded secret. We anticipated a bombshell and the tension mounted toward 10:00 A.M., when the little beige booklet was to be distributed.

There were so many journalists present that it was arranged for the distribution to be made in the auditorium, and there we sat, as if waiting for a movie or play. The rowdy audience treated the introductory remarks of the press office official with ill-concealed impatience and, as the bundles of booklets made their appearance, there was a gradual surge forward, which soon degenerated into a mad rush.

The bearded official tried in vain to curb the riot while the local and foreign journalists swarmed across the stage, grabbing and clawing, as if demented. It became a scene to which only the late Cecil B. DeMille could have done justice. All self-restraint, all decency were abandoned.

I dashed down to the stage and, nipping smartly between the burly form of the local correspondent for the London *Guardian* and the lean figure of the Jerusalem bureau chief of *Newsweek*, I secured my copy.

Sitting outside in the winter sun, I quickly saw that Begin had been "rapped on the knuckles" and that Sharon was the one who had been called on to pay the price. Measures were to be taken against the chief of military intelligence and several senior officers, but the strongest censure was reserved for the chief of staff, who was allowed to retain his position because he was due to wind up his term of office shortly thereafter.

Only later was I able to read the report with the attention it deserved. Concluding that the IDF had taken no direct part in the massacres, the two supreme court judges, Yitzhak Kahan and Aharon Barak, and the retired general, Yona Efrat, took a clear moral stand on the question of Israel's indirect responsibility.

They quoted the Biblical book of Deuteronomy and the Talmud to indicate that Jewish ethics has traditionally accepted the concept of indirect responsibility and noted that in their history the Jews have suffered greatly from pogroms. "The Jewish public's stand has always been that the responsibility for such deeds falls not only on those who rioted and committed the atrocities, but also on those responsible for safety and public order."

The Israeli government and the IDF, says the report, should have been alert to the danger of a Phalangist massacre of Palestinians, particularly after the assassination of Bashir Jemayel.

In its conclusion, the report notes approvingly the efforts made by the IDF to avoid civilian casualties throughout the war and states: "The IDF should continue to foster the consciousness of basic moral obligations which must be kept even in war conditions, without prejudicing the IDF's combat ability. The circumstances of combat require the combatants to be tough ... but the end never justifies the means and the basic ethical and human values must be maintained in the use of arms."

The Lebanon war, which culminated in the massacres of Sabra and Shatila, is a low point in our history, but the wave of protest, which led to the publication of this fine, moral document, is certainly one of the high points.

Those who had demanded an inquiry now pressed for the implementation of the commission's findings, but the country was as bitterly divided over the report as it was over the war. Interested to see what the supporters of the government were saying, I went to Jerusalem's Mahane Yehuda fruit market, a stronghold of Likud support, the day after the report was published.

I did not find a single person there who was pleased about the report, and only one of the fifty-odd people I talked to thought that Sharon should resign. Most of the stall holders are from the Edot and so are more than half the customers.

The mood in the market that afternoon was self-righteous: "The whole matter has been blown up out of proportion. What did we need an inquiry for, anyway? What about the Syrians? What about the Iraqis? They make a fuss only when Jews are involved and we weren't even involved." Such sentiments were repeated over and over again, with slight variations.

One stall holder told me that not only had the IDF not perpetrated the massacres, but it could never have done such a thing. "Bring me an Arab child," he declared dramatically, his arm around the shoulders of an Arab assistant who worked at his fruit stall, "and see if I am capable of harming him!" The others agreed, but with the Arabs it was different, I was told.

My butcher, from whom I have been purchasing meat for a dozen years, is an immigrant from Iraqi Kurdistan. Middle-aged, stocky, grizzled, wearing a skullcap, he has lived in Jerusalem since the 1950s, an almost classical Edot representative. "I am not saying it was right to kill women and children. It does not matter what people or religion; it is forbidden. But we did not do it. Was it the IDF who killed them?" Sharon had served the nation patriotically for thirty years. Why should he be punished for something he didn't do?

They were not alive to the subtlety of "indirect responsibility," nor were they interested in the question of government responsibility for the commission, which it had appointed. As far as they were concerned, the commission was "all Labor party propaganda." They saw it as a plot against them and the Likud. The Likud would win an election with eighty out of one hundred twenty seats, they assured me. Let the Labor party try to have elections now. "That's democracy, isn't it?" asked a dark, powerfully built lad in a tight T-shirt. "Let the people speak!"

The atmosphere was, as always in the market, friendly and good-humored. They all thought they were winning the argument — not only that Sharon should not resign, but that he would not. "Nonsense," I was told. "Nobody's going to resign — you'll see."

Only once was I threatened with violence. An unshaven individual, accompanied by a rather flashy girl, whom I thought he was trying to impress, told me that if I did not get out of the market, he would break my tape recorder. I simply walked down the street and continued my questioning. He did not bother to follow.

For two whole days the cabinet debated the report. Early on, Begin was quoted in the press as saying he wasn't going to fire anybody. Sharon, who had earlier publicly undertaken to honor the committee's conclusions and to resign if any army officer was found remiss in any way, refused to budge. He cunningly suggested delaying the dismissal of the army officers named, on the grounds that they had "served the country patriotically." Everyone — even his supporters admitted it — knew that he was really talking about himself.

While the cabinet debated, a pro-Sharon crowd gathered outside, shouting slogans, and David Magen, a Likud Knesset member, warned, "The street will decide." There was, said the minister of the interior, veteran Yosef Burg, "the smell of a putsch."

Menachem Begin has been described in the Israeli and world media as a "strong leader." It is true that he always got his way in the Herut movement and ousted his political rivals with ease. He also projected a father-figure image, and won the adulation of large sections of the population. Again, he is a fiery and powerful orator. But "strong"? I don't think so.

At Camp David, he shrank from the brave decision to vacate the Sinai settlements, leaving it to the "decision of the Knesset." He even tried for a separate vote on the treaty and the settlements, to evade the stigma of deciding on their abandonment. He failed to give a strong lead on this point.

Jimmy Carter recorded in his autobiography his exasperation at discovering how, after reaching an agreement with Begin (an agreement that the prime minister was perfectly entitled to implement), he had to wait for the whole clause-by-clause agreement to go through the cabinet and the Knesset. No one was going to pin it on Begin alone!

Begin was in fact the king of buck passers. He might as well have had on his desk a sign that said, "The buck never stops here." During the war he took the trouble to distance himself from Sharon. "Sometimes I know about Sharon's decisions before he implements them and sometimes afterward," he stated in a well-placed media leak. His answers to the inquiry commission verged on the pathetic: "I don't know . . . I'm not sure . . . I don't rec-ollect," he repeatedly claimed in his published testimony.

And now, while the nation waited, he said, "I am not going to fire a minister," then sat back to let the others deal with Sharon.

The inquiry commission's report was published on a Tuesday and, on Thursday night, Peace Now decided to mount a counter-demonstration to that of the pro-Sharon crowd outside the prime minister's office. The plan was to march there from the center of town, demonstrating in support of full implementation of the report, which had stated, inter alia, "We have found that the minister of defense bears personal responsibility . . . It is fitting that the minister of defense draw the appropriate personal con-clusions arising out of the defects revealed with regard to the manner in which he discharged the duties of his office." The recommendation goes on to suggest that if Sharon does not re-sign, the prime minister should dismiss him.

That night I was working at the desk of the *Jerusalem Post.* I received a phone call from David Mandel, a subeditor who was not working that night. He had been to the demonstration and was offering a report. Thanking him, I told him that another reporter had been assigned, but I asked him what it had been like. His answer made me sit up. "Scary," he said. I knew that Mandel had attended countless protests — a little shouting would not have worried him.

It wasn't long before the news came in — news that shocked us as much as anything in this war: a grenade had been thrown at the Peace Now demonstrators. We listened incredulously as the radio announced that there were several injured — and one dead.

It was not the first grenade to be thrown in Jerusalem or the first time that people had been killed in our capital. We are fairly inured to it, but this was different — the first political assassination in our three decades.

In a way, what happened later was worse. A grenade can be thrown — maybe was thrown — by a deranged individual, but after the grenade was thrown, an ugly mob continued to attack the Peace Now people. Even the wounded were attacked as they were being rushed off to the hospital.

Some reports depicted the progovernment supporters that night as being solely from the Edot. That is inaccurate. First of all, there were the members of Gush Emunim, who are almost entirely of European origin. Second, there were the seedy supporters of Rabbi Meir Kahane — mostly deranged kids from the United States. Third, I was told by people who were there of middle-aged ladies of European origin who screamed at them, "You have orgies every night. You don't know about suffering: you only care about sex!"

That said, a word about the Edot. In Sdom, by the Dead Sea, I had discovered the depth of their bitterness toward the European Jews, but I had also observed something else: they weren't for the most part physically violent. The Dead Sea dikes project went on for five years, during which several hundred men lived down there on the site in an all-male work camp. During the entire period there was only one attempted murder, and even brawls were rare in the extreme. I have seen more violence on the streets of London than in any Israeli city.

But . . . but, when their prime minister tells them that giving back the West Bank "will endanger every man, woman, and child in Israel," they are not too happy about those who would like to relinquish the occupied territories. When they are told that the opposition wants to give the eternal homeland to the PLO and that the Palestinians are "two-legged beasts," they are not all that friendly toward the opposition.

There has been a "soccer death" in Israel and soccer crowds do turn violent, but again — drawing from my personal experience — less so than in England.

It is only on political issues that the crowds get really violent, and here the prime minister's divisive style was very dangerous. When a Knesset member says openly on television, "Let the street decide!" certain types of people receive the message loud and clear.

I do not charge Menachem Begin with responsibility for the grenade that killed the Peace Now demonstrator, but I do say that the incident of the mob attack on the wounded could have happened only in the hate-filled, divided Israel that his political style created. Yes, indeed, "not the Israel we have seen in the past!"

We still do not know, and may never know, who threw the grenade, but we soon learned the identity of the victim: Emile Grunzweig, a former kibbutznik (of course) and a paratroop officer (of course) who had fought in Lebanon. He was a research student working on a project for Arab youth. Two of his coworkers on the project, Israeli Arabs, were among his bitterest mourners.

On the following day, along with thousands of others, I felt compelled to travel up to Haifa to the funeral of a man whom I had not known. His funeral, under the pines in the old Haifa cemetery beneath Mount Carmel, became a national demonstration. The cars and buses stretched for miles down the road toward Tel Aviv.

Emile's professor spoke simply at the ceremony, appealing for an end to violent speech as well as violent behavior. He asked for an end to the use of such phrases as "stab in the back," "poison," and "fifth column," which had been used often by government supporters in this war.

Then it was the turn of Shlomo Goren, chief rabbi at the time, a man famous for his nationalist beliefs. When he spoke, he was interrupted by shouts of anger and bitterness, and when he declaimed, "We do not know whose hand struck you down, Emile," a man standing near me was unable to contain himself and shouted,

"*Your* hand struck him down!" Such was the hatred abroad in the land that day.

Around the time that Emile was being buried, Ariel Sharon, who had at last agreed to quit, was speaking to a luncheon meeting of Tel Aviv lawyers. We saw him that night on television. He apparently chose the occasion to tell amusing stories and crack jokes. We did not hear any of the jokes or the stories, but we could see the assembled attorneys — to their everlasting shame — laughing their heads off.

4
The Heart of the Matter

When the Israeli chief of staff spoke to his troops in Beirut in the third month of the war, he told them that they were "fighting the battle for the Land of Israel." And he was right, for at the heart of the conflict between Jews and Arabs in the Middle East is the struggle for possession of the land, which the Jews call Israel and the Arabs call Palestine.

Each side describes the conflict in the way that best reflects on its cause. Thus, for the Israelis it is a "struggle for the right to exist"; for the Arabs it is a "battle to regain the stolen land."

When two people want the same thing, the one who wants it most usually gets it; when two people want the same thing very much, there has to be a compromise. The Jews and the Arabs have never managed to achieve a compromise about the land between the Mediterranean and the river Jordan because both sides believe so fervently in the justice of their cause.

The fact that the Jews have Israel is an indication that their determination is the greater; the refusal of the Arabs to accept defeat (and the resultant continuing conflict) is an indication that the Arab determination is pretty strong, too.

The Middle East problem has defied the efforts of both its protagonists and outsiders to solve it. It has been correctly described as "intractable." The dictionary tells us that intractable means "not easily dealt with," and this definition is not one that precludes hope for the future.

The problem is one of missed trains. In 1949, after the War of Independence, the Israelis were waiting at the station, but the Arabs were not ready to climb on board. They thought that if they persisted in their hostility, they might still be able to destroy the new Jewish state. While the Israelis were overwhelmed with relief that they had achieved statehood, they also knew that it was less than they had desired. To them it seemed the time for compromise: Israel would exist, but parts of the Land of Israel would have to be forfeited.

In 1967 the Israelis felt the same way, but more so. Now there was something practical, actual territory in their possession, to offer the Arab side. Once again the Arabs missed the train.

When Anwar Sadat came to Jerusalem in 1977, ten years and one war later, it was the Israelis who missed the train, together with the Palestinians and the other Arabs. Sadat caught his train and got back Sinai in return for a peace treaty. He tried to make it a package deal to solve the whole Middle East problem, but he was let down by his fellow Arabs and by the Israelis. The Israeli train had gone too far down the tracks and was prepared only to shunt back to the Sinai station, quite a long way, but not far enough. In any case, the Palestinians were not waiting at the West Bank–Gaza station.

In 1983 the Israeli train was firmly halted at the Sinai station. Thus far and no farther, said Menachem Begin's Israeli government, believing that if it held on just a little longer, the whole Land of Israel could be its possession forever.

The Arab train was moving backward and forward between Ramallah and Tel Aviv. There were several hands on the wheel and none of them seemed all that sure in which direction to point the engine. On the Arab side there were hints, indications, tendencies toward the acceptance of the 1949-model Israel, but the Israelis would not shunt back that far.

The aim must be to get both trains to the same station at the same time. The Israeli train must shunt backward some of the way, and the Arab train must drive forward decisively. The West Bankers must elbow aside the other drivers, whether the Arab states or the PLO, and take charge of their own engine once and for all.

The Jewish people have lived in the Land of Israel from the time of Abraham, around 2000 B.C., and, despite three periods of exile, there has never been a time since when some Jews were not living there.

Jewish sovereignty was ended by the Romans, who, after a series of revolts against their administration, expelled large numbers of Jews and renamed the country Paelestina. They also destroyed Jerusalem and renamed it Aelia Capitolina. The name Jerusalem returned, but the name Paelestina, later Palestine, after the Philistines who for a time inhabited the coastal plain, stuck. The country was conquered by the Arabs, when they swept up out of the Arabian peninsula in A.D. 732, and became part of the vast Arab empire, which was eventually superseded by that of the Ottoman Turks.

During the two thousand years of their dispersion, the Jews retained a unique bond with their land, praying daily for their return. Regarding themselves as being "in exile," they continued to observe their religious festivals according to the seasons of their distant land. Over the years, numbers of Jews returned to their homeland, supplementing those who had remained, but since Roman times they had always been a minority.

The modern Zionist movement, which aimed at the mass return of Jews to their ancestral land, began in the age of imperialism but drew its inspiration from the European national liberation movements of the late nineteenth century. Its opponents have seen Zionism as part of European imperialism; Zionism sees itself as the Jewish national liberation movement.

It was a modern response to the repeated persecution that Jews had suffered over the centuries. Confined to the ghetto since medieval times, the Jews discovered that emancipation did not bring an end to persecution. Emerging from the ghetto, the Jew met prejudice and hatred.

In 1895, Alfred Dreyfus, a Jewish captain in the French army, was found guilty of treason and sent to Devil's Island. Although the verdict was subsequently overturned and Dreyfus was released, the case unleashed a wave of anti-Semitism in France, the most enlightened of European countries.

A young assimilated Jewish journalist from Vienna, Theodor Herzl, sent by his newspaper to cover the case, was shattered to the core. He promptly sat down and wrote a pamphlet, *The Jewish State*, arguing that the Jews must return en masse to their ancient homeland, and two years later convened the first Zionist Congress. The response was overwhelming, particularly among the Jews of Russia, where they still suffered from pogroms in which their lives and property were menaced.

Herzl was aware that the ancient homeland was now inhabited by Arabs. In his visionary novel, *Altneuland*, he describes a Jewish president and an Arab vice president ruling a sort of binational state. However, the Zionist pioneers, involved in clashes with the local population, did not see them in nationalist terms, viewing them rather as "bandits" when they were attacked by them.

The Arab national movement, founded in Damascus, was one step behind Zionism. Nahum Goldmann, one of the more perceptive Zionist leaders, once said that if Zionism had arrived fifty years earlier, the Jewish state would have been established without too much difficulty. If it had been conceived fifty years later, it would never have gotten off the ground. It was the almost simultaneous development of the two nationalisms — Jewish and Arab — that led to an inevitable clash.

Palestinian nationalism, of course, came much later and is the creation of Israel. In 1948 the Arabs could easily have established a Palestinian state in the West Bank and Gaza, as envisaged by the United Nations when it voted for partition in 1947, but Egypt hung on to Gaza and Transjordan annexed the West Bank and changed its name to Jordan.

If the pogroms in Russia had acted as a spur to Zionism, the Nazi Holocaust converted the Jewish national movement into a raging need. After Hitler, there was no question of compromising on Jewish statehood, despite the implacable Arab opposition.

The case for Zionism was eloquently put to the Anglo-American committee of inquiry on Palestine in 1945 by Chaim Weizmann, the aging leader of the Zionist movement: "Injustice there is going to be . . . There may be some slight injustice politically if Palestine is made a Jewish state, but individually the Arabs will not suffer." He went on: "The position of the Arabs as a people is secure. Their national sentiments can find full expression in Cairo, Damascus, and Baghdad . . . I think that the line of least injustice demands that we should be given our chance."

The Jews accepted the idea of partitioning the land; the Arabs rejected it. The British wound up their mandate and the Jews declared the State of Israel in their part of Palestine.

The armies of five Arab states invaded and, in the ensuing war the Jews, while losing some territory and several villages, mostly advanced and secured rather more than the UN had awarded them. Some six hundred thousand Palestinians fled from their homes during the fighting and became refugees in Gaza, the West Bank, Jordan, Lebanon, and Syria. The Arab states deliberately refrained from absorbing these refugees and continued to demand that they return to their homes.

Four of the five invading states (Iraq was the exception) signed armistice agreements with Israel in 1949, but they did not recognize or accept the Jewish state. They continued to declare that they were "in a state of war" with Israel and sent saboteurs across the border with increasing frequency.

In the early years of the state, some seven hundred thousand Jews from North Africa, Yemen, Iraq, and other Middle Eastern countries, came to live in Israel. Israel has always regarded this double exodus as a population exchange, but the Arab side never accepted this view. There was no Palestinian national movement in the early years; the talk was of the Arab refugees being permitted to return home—not of the creation of a Palestinian state.

Palestinian nationalism began in the late 1950s, with the establishment of cells of the *Fatah* in Kuwait and Qatar in 1958. The Palestine Liberation Organization was established in 1965, although it became important only after the Six Day War.

My own first acquaintance with Palestinian nationalism came in 1965, when I met Mansur Kardosh, secretary of the Israeli-Arab nationalist movement, *El-Ard*, "the land." The movement was declared illegal, on the grounds that it was opposed to the existence of the State of Israel and, in the 1965 general election, Kardosh was "exiled" for about a month to Arad, where I was living at the time, to prevent his exercising an influence in his native Nazareth.

Mansur Kardosh is tall, gray-haired, fair-skinned, and dresses informally in the Israeli style, but slightly more elegantly than most Israelis, in well-pressed gray bush shirt and linen trousers. He is fluent in English and pretends not to know Hebrew. A warm, friendly person, with a pleasant manner and ready smile, he responded immediately to our invitation to lunch. In his rather paranoid mood, a result of his exile to Arad and the disbanding of his movement, he rather exaggerated my "courage" in inviting him.

We have subsequently visited him in his Nazareth home and our friendship has been preserved, despite strong disagreement over politics. He is a strong supporter of the PLO, but when I first met him I had not heard of that organization. We began arguing at our first meeting and have been arguing fiercely but amicably ever since. I find that we can have a rational discussion about Zionism or Palestinian nationalism, but when I criticize an act of terrorism by the PLO, or he condemns the confiscation of Arab land in Galilee, the going gets rougher.

In 1965 I felt some sympathy for his ideas but thought them wildly unrealistic. The Palestinians, he told me, were a nation. It was untrue that his El-Ard movement was not prepared to accept Israel. Israel was an incontrovertible fact and he was a realist, but the Palestinians were entitled to a state in the remaining parts of western Palestine. At the time he felt there should be a return to the 1947 partition plan, which involved Israel's giving up territory. In 1983 he was prepared to accept the 1949 armistice borders, but he had two reservations.

The first was that there should be "some autonomy" for Nazareth and other Israeli Arab towns and villages. The second was that the Palestinians should have the right to "bring up the question of a secular state," at regular intervals, "for a hundred years if necessary."

The "secular state" for Muslims, Christians, and Jews, to replace Israel, has been the official policy of the PLO since soon after the Six Day War. Previously, the Arab states had said clearly that the Jews "should be driven into the sea." When Yasir Arafat became head of the PLO, he took up the more moderate line of the secular state.

Mansur Kardosh has been prepared to renounce violence and look on the secular state as an aspiration, but the PLO has never moved as far as his position. If it had done so, it might have been a credible negotiating partner for solving the dispute. The PLO's charter, known as the Palestine National Covenant, has never been repealed.

Article 6 of the covenant states that "Jews who were living permanently in Palestine until the beginning of the Zionist invasion will be considered Palestinians." (In his speech to the UN general assembly in 1974, Arafat said that the Zionist invasion began in 1881.) Article 9 states that "armed struggle is the only way to liberate Palestine," and article 15 that "it is a national duty . . . to purge the Zionist presence from Palestine." Article 19 describes the UN partition resolution on Palestine as "fundamentally null and void."

The most that the PLO has done to repeal this covenant is to adopt an interim position stating that the PLO was prepared to establish a state on any "liberated land," but it was made very clear that this was only a step in the direction of the restoration of all of Palestine to Arab rule.

The PLO position was not mere talk; it suited action to words. Operating initially from Jordan, it organized a continuous series of attacks — mines, grenades, and shootings — in Israel, the West Bank, and Gaza. In these operations more Arabs than Jews were killed, but the attacks were directed at the "Zionist enemy" and the PLO gleefully claimed credit for them.

In 1970, after they were expelled from Jordan by King Hussein, who feared that they would take over his country, the PLO continued its acts of terrorism and sabotage, extending them to targets outside Israel. A Swiss airplane was blown up in midair while on its way to Israel; eleven Israeli Olympic athletes were murdered in Munich; Christian pilgrims were gunned down at Lydda Airport by a Japanese gunman acting on PLO orders; letter bombs were sent to Israelis and Jews all over the world.

In 1978 the PLO brought off a spectacular raid in which a gang hijacked a bus and drove it down toward Tel Aviv. In the subsequent shoot-out, thirty-seven Israelis were killed. The coastal road massacre led directly to the Litani operation, during which the PLO was pushed out of South Lebanon. Three years later it was back, making life impossible for Israelis living in Kiryat Shmona, Misgav Am, and other northern settlements.

When the Israel Defense Forces invaded Lebanon in June 1982, they discovered considerable documentary evidence that the PLO planned to continue its harassment of the northern towns and villages. One order to an artillery unit of the PLO listed thirteen targets, of which only one was military. The others, including two Lebanese villages in the south, were all civilian settlements.

The document was addressed to PLO, the United Command Artillery, and marked "Top secret and most urgent." There follows a list of the targets and the times to open fire.

There is no question that the PLO was not planning to play dominoes on Israel's northern border; it was being true to its thesis that "armed struggle is the only way to liberate Palestine."

When Israel drove into Lebanon, its aim was to smash the PLO and thereby, it was hoped, destroy Palestinian nationalism. So it was quite right to describe the fighting in Beirut as part of the "battle for the Land of Israel." The question that remains is whether the war brought advances for either side. In my view it brought distinct disadvantages both to Israel and the PLO. But if the situation is handled the right way, it could yet bring advantages to both sides.

As in 1945, Israel can make out a good case against a Palestinian state. Weizmann pointed out that there were then seven Arab states and no Jewish state. Today there is a Jewish state, but the Arabs have twenty-two nations. Furthermore, the Arabs have used the whole Palestinian question as a stick with which to beat Israel. I do not think that the denial of Palestinian statehood is the world's greatest injustice, but it is an injustice and it does harm to Israel's character as a state.

Israeli rule in the West Bank and Gaza started out well. Moshe Dayan's combination of firmness and liberalism worked as a temporary solution. After the initial shock of the conquest by Israel, there were numerous acts of sabotage, which were countered with arrests, expulsions, trials, administrative detention, and the blowing up of suspects' houses.

Apart from the fight against terrorism, there was little interference in the daily lives of the citizens and military rule was not too oppressive. Although they were not permitted to organize politically, the citizens of the West Bank and Gaza were freer than they had been under Jordanian rule. They were allowed to publish newspapers and to speak out on political matters, provided their words and writings were not judged to be "incitement." They were permitted to come into Israel to work and to cross the river Jordan to the Arab countries. Their trade with the Arab world actually increased at first.

The inhabitants of the territories benefited economically from the Israeli occupation. Since 1967, the Gross National Product in the areas has increased by 13 percent a year, per capita income went up by 11 percent in real terms, and private consumption rose at the rate of 7 percent per year.

Some 20 percent of households were connected to the electricity grid in 1967; today about 73 percent of houses in the West Bank and over 90 percent in Gaza have electricity. There were about seven thousand vehicles in the territories; today the number is thirty-eight thousand.

There has been a revolution in farming. Agricultural production per acre has doubled, as modern methods of irrigation and fertilization were introduced. There are seven times as many tractors today as there were in 1967.

The number of teachers and classrooms has increased; today 90 percent of children up to the age of eighteen attend school, where in 1967 the figure was less than 60 percent. There were no universities in the West Bank and Gaza; today there are five.

Of course, the universities have become centers of political awareness and have consequently been the scenes of clashes between students and IDF troops. Although they have sometimes been harassed and often closed down for periods of time, the universities continue to develop and flourish.

In the early years of the occupation the IDF behaved with relative humanity, but, even then, I discovered when I served in the Gaza Strip that there was no such thing as a "humane occupation." The very nature of the task we were called on to perform was dehumanizing. It was impossible to take the necessary measures against terrorism without degrading the inhabitants.

We challenged the Arabs in the dark alleys of their towns day by day and night by night. We set up roadblocks and searched their cars. We strode into their cafés to interrupt their evenings of dominoes and cards. We lined them up against the wall and examined their documents while their coffee grew cold. We surrounded their neighborhoods and searched their homes and their bodies. It was absolutely necessary to do all this, for there were acts of terrorism: explosive charges were detonated, grenades were thrown — not to mention rocks.

The climax came when we shot an old woman. An honest

mistake on our part, it was perpetrated on a dark night, near the shore at a location used for smuggling in arms by sea. The woman, even though she should not have been there, was innocent, and we killed her.

On the whole, I was not too distressed by the attitude of my fellow soldiers. There were cases of brutality, but they were stopped by the officers and were the exception rather than the rule. I perceived that most soldiers who acted nastily were nervous rather than sadistic.

There was some loose talk about how we should be tougher with the locals and knock them around a bit, but this was mostly among soldiers far from the action — mechanics and cooks. The fiercest soldier by far was the camp barber. I have talked to other soldiers about this subject and we all agree. Years of military service indicate that the front-line soldiers are the most humane; the heroes who want to shoot and fight and kill are those who spend their time safely out of harm's way. In the Lebanon war, the joke was that in Tel Aviv the reservist's chant was "Begin-Begin!" But the nearer he got to Rosh Hanikra, the less enthu siastic his chanting became. Actually inside Lebanon, his chant changed to "Begin, go home!"

In 1970 I was most worried about what the effect would be on me. Scared stiff at the outset of my first term of service in Gaza, I gradually became more confident as I learned the job and gained experience. I once caught sight of myself in a shop window: there I was, a former antinuclear marcher, with uniform, helmet, flak jacket, ammunition belt, and weapon at the ready. Was the self-confidence in my walk turning into a swagger?

When I subsequently served in Gaza again, I could see how the area had been rebuilt; the people were better clothed, the children more friendly and less afraid of us. But Gaza was not Israel, and the masses of children pouring out of school at midday were not Israelis.

Since 1967 there has been — along with the improvement in standards of living — a deterioration. There is no way that the behavior of IDF troops can be described as "humane" today, particularly after Ariel Sharon became defense minister.

Richard Crossman was right when he wrote to Abba Eban, who was once — it seems a century ago — Israel's foreign minister, "The Arabs can survive a decade of Jewish military domination. The Israel you and I believe in can't." In the same letter, published in the *New Statesman* in 1970, Crossman wrote, "Your hold over the West Bank must grow ever more oppressive, the longer it lasts." Even earlier, Professor Yeshaiahu Leibowitz, a religious Israeli dove, had written, "The corruption typical of any colonial regime will also affect the State of Israel."

Crossman and Leibowitz were right. Early in 1983 an IDF officer and six soldiers were tried for assaulting and mistreating Arabs in the Hebron area the previous year. The fact that the soldiers were put on trial is encouraging, but this came about only because of complaints by reserve soldiers, members of Peace Now, who were serving in the West Bank.

Even more disturbing than the actions themselves were the attitudes of the defense minister and the chief of staff, which emerged during the trial. The defense counsel for the accused stated, "At this trial, to my sorrow, in addition to the accused, the entire IDF, including the highest ranks, is on trial for its policy in the territories."

In an official memorandum, quoted at the trial, the chief of staff ordered officers to "use the means of punishing the parents" of troublemakers, arrest suspects for eighteen days without trial, release them, and then rearrest them. Appearing as a witness, Chief of Staff Etan was unrepentant. Punishing parents for the actions of their children "works very well with Arabs," he told the court. He confirmed that he had ordered arrests and rearrests of suspects. "It's perfectly legal," he remarked.

Asked whether a rude gesture on the part of an Arab youth justified a beating, he said it depended on the circumstances. "If the soldier is of, say, Iraqi origin and he thinks the finger is raised in an insulting manner and strikes out with a club and the Arab lies on the ground, I agree with his judgment."

There is no doubt that with the replacement of Sharon as defense minister by Moshe Arens and the appointment of a new chief of staff, the situation on the ground has improved. The current military commander on the West Bank, a combat veteran with an impeccable record, is making a genuine attempt to prevent this sort of conduct and to investigate any report of brutal or unjust behavior on the part of his soldiers, but the situation will inevitably lead to some abuses.

Standards today are not the same as those in the early years of the occupation. When I was serving in Gaza in 1970, a Druze scout serving with our unit beat a local lad with a cane because, he said, the boy had been insulting. He was harshly rebuked and taken off patrol duty. The Druze was terribly humiliated; nevertheless, he was told, IDF soldiers just do not behave that way.

Gaza 1970 was far more dangerous than the West Bank today, where rowdy youths throw stones and an occasional kerosene bottle at IDF patrols. In Gaza, during my first tour of duty, there were genuine terrorist cells, which carried out armed attacks on soldiers and civilians. One soldier in my battalion was killed and several were wounded in such incidents.

I remember standing in the town square of Khan Yunis near Gaza in the center of a stone-throwing mob. My officer was hit on the hand by a rock as large as a brick. We called the regional command by radio; it took twenty minutes before we got authorization to make a few arrests, "without undue violence."

It was drummed into us night and day that we must try not to humiliate the local citizen. "Honor him and suspect him," we were told. Not all citizens are terrorists — most of them are peaceful people who must be allowed to go about their business unmolested. The orders were given in writing and repeated verbally.

The instructions about opening fire were particularly strict. We were not to fire unless fired on. Even then we were to aim carefully at the attackers and do all we could not to hit civilians. These days one often reads of soldiers opening fire "at the legs of stone-throwing demonstrators," and killing them.

The most disturbing statement made at the trial was one in

the then chief of staff's memorandum, which said, "The residents of the Jewish settlements have to carry arms and open fire when they are attacked. This should be made clear and publicized among the Arab residents."

I am grateful to the chief of staff for making the price of remaining in the occupied territories so clear. Nothing illustrates the degeneration of our standards more clearly than his statement about the settlers. The West Bank settlers, and in particular the activists who belong to Gush Emunim, are always proclaiming their desire for "coexistence with their Arab neighbors." On the ground the situation is very different.

Visiting the Jewish settlements in the West Bank with Matti Drobless, head of the World Zionist Organization settlement department, is an almost surrealistic experience. One can spend a whole day in the West Bank without realizing that Arabs live there. "I am concerned about the Jewish problem; I don't have time for the Arab problem," he admits. "My concern is that more than half the Jewish people is still in exile." The burly, snub-nosed, gray-haired Drobless came to Israel from Argentina in 1949. A long-time member of the Likud, he points proudly to the red-roofed villas set among the beautiful hills of Samaria and says that the government has pre-empted any return of the area to foreign rule. "I feel privileged to be part of an administration which has ensured the eternal sovereignty of the Jewish people in Judea and Samaria," he says. He may be a little premature.

The government has made it cheap and attractive to settle in the territories, and new towns supplement the more idealistic Gush Emunim villages. In 1983 a journalist colleague exchanged his stuffy two-room Jerusalem apartment for a five-and-a-half-room duplex at Maale Adumim, a new settlement ten miles east of Jerusalem. He happens to be a government supporter, but Peace Now tells me it also has members with addresses and phone numbers in that community. It is simply too tempting. An Israeli family that dreams of a private house can now achieve the impossible by moving to one of the new settlements.

Nevertheless, there is a limit to the number of Israelis who can afford a villa, even in the territories. The reserve will soon run out. There are only some thirty thousand Jews in the occupied territories alongside more than a million Arabs. The government aims to double the number in two years and to get to one hundred thousand in three or four. Maybe. But a million by 1990 — or even by the end of the century — is a pipe dream. Settling people takes time. Israel is only now completing the settlement of the immigrants of the 1950s.

I was a founder-citizen of the town of Arad in the Negev in 1962. Admittedly farther away from the center of the country than the towns of Samaria and Judea and consequently less attractive, Arad is nevertheless Israel's most successful development town: well planned, attractive, good climate, adequate educational and recreational facilities, many job opportunities. Our aim was to get to fifty thousand in ten to fifteen years. In twenty years Arad grew from zero to . . . fifteen thousand. Moving people takes time.

Let's take Ariel, the largest town in Samaria. When I visited there in 1978 with Ariel Sharon and a party of American Zionists, we were told that there were eight hundred families in the town. Five years later, on my tour with Drobless, the number of families had "grown" to three hundred!

Interestingly, the doves and the Arabs are alarmed. The government and the Gush have managed to create an illusion of mass settlement. They have not missed a trick. Drobless took us to Emmanuel, a complete town being built for ultra-Orthodox, non-Zionist Jews, who are attracted by the cheap land and easy loans. They only just about accept the State of Israel, let alone Greater Israel, but they are settling there. It was unreal to see the black-suited, bearded figures, with their gaiters and broad-brimmed hats, picking their way through the mud and boulders against the spectacular backdrop of the Samaria Mountains. It looked like a scene out of a movie by Mel Brooks.

In the Gush Emunim settlement of Ofra, a young American girl, wearing the long skirt and head scarf of the observant, told us that her settlement was based on self-labor. "We don't want the Arabs to do our dirty work for us while we become a leisured class," she declared.

Later I returned to Ofra for a chat with Yisrael Harel, head of the Council of Jewish Settlements in Judea and Samaria. To reach Ofra, you drive along winding roads, through groves of olive trees, and past picturesque Arab villages of gray stone. There is, in fact, an Arab olive grove within the "security fence" of Ofra. The Arab owners must ask permission to come in to tend their trees, and the only way in is through the main gate of the Jewish village.

Harel, a stocky, bespectacled man with the usual knitted skull-cap, is by far the most persuasive settler spokesman I have met. Formerly a journalist with the afternoon paper *Yediot Ahronot*, he now presides over an authority representing a dozen regional and municipal councils in the West Bank and Gaza.

Harel was confident about the future of the West Bank as part of Israel. The natural Arab increase since 1967 had been close to zero, he noted, largely because of emigration. Jewish immigration could be increased, he thought. Gush Emunim had started recruiting actively in America and this effort would soon show results. Building was proceeding at a great pace, he maintained. He was not worried about the unrest among the local population. Stone throwing could be dangerous, even fatal, "but we can live with it."

He conceded that there was a problem with the local population, but he foresaw a number of options for solving it. Support was growing for a functional-federal solution, in which the Arabs of the West Bank would vote for parliament in Amman and find their political self-expression in Jordan. Living in Ofra had taught him patience, he remarked. "We do not have to achieve everything in this generation." It was enough, he asserted, to ensure that Judea and Samaria remained in Jewish hands. Future generations could worry about the remainder of the Land of Israel. "We should certainly not go to war for Transjordan," he said.

Harel dismissed the argument that dominating a million Arabs was contrary to the Torah. "All this talk about freedom and national self-determination is an import from Western liberalism," he told me. "It has nothing to do with Judaism; the Torah is not moralist — it contains commandments, telling us what we must do." He was not insensitive to world opinion. It was important to take into consideration what other people thought, but Israel had to get its priorities right. Security and national rights of the Jewish people came first.

Harel denied that Arabs were being dispossessed. Only three hundred thousand *dunams* (75,000 acres) — 5 percent of all West Bank land — was being put aside for settlement, he noted. Later I checked with Plia Albeck, the government official investigating the land question for the State Attorney's Office. She confirmed Harel's figure but admitted that about half the land in the West Bank had been designated as "state land," meaning that it is potentially at the disposal of the Israel government.

In previous years Arab landowners successfully challenged the Jewish takeover of their land in Israel's supreme court, so the government has learned its lesson and now builds on "state land." It has encouraged the private purchase of land in the West Bank, but these operations ran into difficulties and for a time were suspended.

Harel claimed that the vast majority of the settlers disassociated themselves from the vigilante acts of a few "extremists." He is being disingenuous. When an illegal settlement group of Meir Kahane's far-right group was removed from its site, Gush Emunim leaders tried to help them find another location. Hanan Porat admitted to me that this was so. "I don't agree with their methods," he said, "but I will do anything to help any group of Jews which wants to settle the Land of Israel." According to reports in the media, Porat has used his status as a Knesset member to intervene with the police and persuade them to drop charges against suspected vigilantes.

Kahane, a rabbi formerly from the United States, has a small group of followers, almost all from America. They are not representative of anything or anyone in Israel, but Gush Emunim's ambivalent attitude toward them casts doubt on the sincerity of the Gush claim that it really wants peaceful coexistence on the West Bank.

When Israel took over the West Bank and Gaza in 1967, the municipalities were dominated by the traditional powerful families and clans. The military government facilitated new local elections, and in 1976 a new leadership took over in the area. It was the first time that women were permitted to vote and, generally, the poll was the freest ever held in the region, but it was not good for Israel. Candidates who supported the PLO were elected in almost every West Bank town.

Shimon Peres, today leader of the Labor opposition, had by then taken over from Moshe Dayan as defense minister and he was widely blamed for the "PLO triumph" in the 1976 municipal elections, which brought such men as Bassam Shak'a and Kerim Khallaf to power.

My most vivid memory of the actual poll, which I covered for Israel radio, was of the women voters. The Jordanian law had been amended to give them the vote. Various property and other regulations were similarly amended to make the elections more democratic.

There had been some doubts as to whether the newly enfranchised voters would come to the polls, particularly the women. They came. There were young, elegant ladies in modern dress —some in slacks and blouses. There were sophisticated, middle-aged matrons who might have walked out of Europe in the 1930s. There were others in the traditional black Arab *galabiya* tunics and keffiye headdresses, some with tattoos on their faces, many veiled in traditional Muslim fashion. They swarmed to the polling stations in a never-ending stream. They seemed to demand their right to vote as they waited patiently in the hot sun. The polling booths had to remain open for an extra two hours to meet the rush. It was later alleged that the PLO had used intimidation to secure the victory of the radical mayors. Interviews conducted both before and after the poll convinced me that they had majority support.

The day after the results had been declared, I drove high up into the pine-covered hills above Ramallah to speak to Kerim Khallaf, one of the few radicals who had been in office before the election. He had been re-elected with a thumping majority.

Khallaf, tall, suave, with swept-back, graying hair and mustache, was still dressed in his dark, formal suit, but he had loosened his tie. Relaxed, sitting almost horizontally in a deep armchair, he spoke more freely than he ever had. There was a remarkable number of empty whiskey bottles in his lounge, and it may be that some of the drink had found its way down his throat — he is a Christian, not a Muslim, so alcohol is not forbidden him.

The previous day, before the election, he had been tense and nervous, refusing all interviews. If his bully boys were busy ensuring the result, he clearly was not confident of their efficacy. Now he was all smiles and repeatedly referred to me as his "dear friend." (I had, in fact, interviewed him only once previously.)

He fenced elegantly with my questions as to whether the election had been free and fair. If he admitted that the elections were fair, he pointed out, it would be used as propaganda by the Israelis. He did not know whether it had been fair or not, but he noted that two of his nationalist colleagues (from neighboring El-Bireh and Hebron) had been expelled before the poll, so the Israelis had already "interfered in the elections." He did admit that his fear that the ballot boxes would be tampered with had apparently been unjustified.

I asked him whether, as mayor, he would continue to cooperate with the military government. He replied that he had tried cooperation "for the good of the people," but the military governor had not wanted to give services. "His aim is to kick the people off its land and bring in Jews from Russia and Europe to settle on our property."

Question: When the West Bank was part of Jordan, did the municipality have a better relationship with the government?

Answer: I am not going to talk about that. It is better not to be with Jordan and not to be with the Israelis. It is better to establish our own Palestinian state.

The Israelis were treating the West Bank population "brutally," he told me.

"You hate every Arab," he said. "You hate mankind. The Jews hate mankind; they only love each other!"

"Do you really believe that?" I asked.

"When I was a student at Cairo University, I had many Jewish friends," he replied. "They used to think like Arabs, or like anyone else, but the Israelis are different. Your thoughts are different from others' in the whole world. You just love yourselves and you hate the others. That is our feeling." (I still have a transcript of the interview and I have rendered the direct quotes verbatim.)

Maybe, he continued, Israel would be occupied one day, by the Russians or the Chinese, and then I would know what it was like. He hoped that this would not happen to me, but one never knew. As I left, he threw his arm affectionately around my shoulders and again called me "my dear friend." But, he added, "You do hate humanity — that is your fate, that is your complex."

It pains me to record that some time after his election, he was blown up by a car bomb and lost a foot. A similar attack was made on his colleague from Nablus, Bassam Shak'a, and he lost two legs. The perpetrators of the attacks on the mayors have never been discovered, but Rabbi Moshe Levinger told me quite openly, "We all feel much safer," following the incidents.

Kerim Khallaf, Bassam Shak'a, and most of the other West Bank mayors were dismissed after they refused to cooperate with the new "civil administration" established by Ariel Sharon in what was supposed to be an initial step toward the "full autonomy" promised by the Begin government.

The mayors felt that if they cooperated with anything other than a military administration they would be accepting permanent Israeli rule. The situation has become positively Orwellian, since the "civil" administration has in fact involved the appointment of Israeli army officers as mayors of most West Bank towns.

The government also established "village leagues" based on the village councils, which are supposedly more conservative than the towns. It was hoped that they would form an alternative West Bank leadership, which would accept autonomy.

Muhammad Naser, leader of the Hebron area leagues, formed a party called the Palestinian Democratic Peace Movement. Its platform was "the recognition of Israel and the achievement of Palestinian rights through negotiation." Naser was rewarded by being removed from office by the head of the civil administration, Brigadier Shlomo Iliya, which casts considerable doubt on the seriousness with which the government regards its own autonomy proposals.

In fact, most West Bankers to whom I have talked regard the village league leaders as "illiterates," at best, or as "quislings," at worst. There does not seem to be a prospect of an alternative leadership to the PLO here, even if one were allowed to emerge.

The West Bank mayors, before their dismissal, were a more promising prospect, but, unfortunately, they always insisted that "the PLO is the sole representative of the Palestinian people."

The PLO has been a disappointment to Israelis who favor a genuine dialogue with the Palestinians. Even in the light of the Lebanon war, the organization has not managed to soften its stand. Sympathizers with the Palestinian cause often point out that Yasir Arafat cannot afford to moderate his stand because he would be assassinated by more extreme elements if he did so. It is not clear to me how this argument is supposed to reassure Israelis who would like a dialogue with him.

During the siege of Beirut, Arafat talked to several Israeli journalists, and here again his remarks fell short of what is necessary for the opening of a dialogue. He told journalist Amnon Kapeleuk of *Yediot Ahronot*, "We are prepared to make contact with anyone who recognizes our right to self-determination." But when Kapeleuk asked him whether he would recognize Israel, Arafat replied that the current Israeli leadership was on record as saying that even if the PLO did recognize Israel, it would not negotiate with it. It was the PLO, he argued, that needed recognition from Israel, not the other way around.

When Kapeleuk explained that many Israelis were concerned that the PLO would not be satisfied with a West Bank–Gaza state, Arafat did not bother to issue a denial. He merely noted that Israel was a strong country and that it would take a Palestinian state "twenty years to get on its feet."

When the Palestine National Council met in Algiers in February 1983, there was more of this sort of double talk. Hopeful observers pointed out that the PNC did not reject the Reagan plan outright, but there was still nothing concrete to get hold of. Arafat held extensive consultations with King Hussein to discover whether the king might represent him in a diplomatic initiative; in the end he let Hussein down and nothing came of it. Arafat's position in the PLO — even his own Fatah organization — was gravely threatened by his going even that far.

How far has Arafat actually gone? Let us examine this extract from the Kapeleuk interview in Beirut:

Kapeleuk: The [Palestine National] covenant gives ammunition to your foes. It discounts Israel's right to exist and says that armed struggle is the only way to establish your state.
Arafat: We have already decided that armed struggle is not the only way. People have tried to interpret the covenant in a biased way. I suggest we call a symposium of Jews, Palestinians, and other Arabs after the war to examine this question. The Palestinians have changed their perceptions in recent years. We did not know how to put our message across to the Israelis.

It is wrong to say that Arafat has been trying the "diplomatic method." He has never really tried it. He has been a disaster for the Palestinians. True, he has succeeded in putting their message across in the free world. His unshaven face beneath its red keffiye has become the symbol of Palestine, but he has also succeeded in embroiling his countrymen in murderous military conflicts — with Jordan in 1970, with Syria in 1976, with Israel in 1982, and again with Syria in 1983. In each of these battles, the Palestinians lost many lives and gained nothing.

Whether Arafat survives or not has become increasingly irrelevant. He may try again to reach agreement with King Hussein and move toward a political solution. Now that the split in the PLO has been forced on him, this would be easier than in the past. I would not like to reject Arafat entirely. He does have a measure of support in the West Bank, particularly since his battles with the Syrians; but in my view the West Bankers should outgrow him. Without him, they will have a far better chance to persuade Israel to take them seriously. His disastrous record of misjudgment and failure is a good enough reason to dump him.

The time has come for the West Bankers themselves to take charge of their own fate. It will not be easy, but then, we have seen that the problem is intractable, which means "not easily dealt with."

Although most people you talk to in the West Bank say they support the PLO, they do not in fact support its extreme positions. I have no doubt that a majority of West Bankers would be happy to see Israel disappear, but not more than a handful really believe that this is possible. They are all too aware of Israel's strength. Half an hour's conversation with "radical" students at Birzet, or any other West Bank university, elicits the knowledge that they envisage their dreamed-of Palestinian state alongside Israel — not instead of it.

There was a time when Palestinian nationalists in the West Bank used to look on the return of King Hussein as the worst thing that could happen. Begin managed to change this: today most West Bankers prefer the return of Hussein to the continuation of Israeli rule.

"King Hussein is the ruler of a medieval regime," explained

Muhammad Abu-Shilbaye, an East Jerusalem writer and teacher. "Hussein put us in jail for our views. He beat us, killed us, hanged us, but his Bedouin never came and said, 'This is our land,' as the Israelis do. They say that this is the Land of Israel and we are foreigners. One day we will find ourselves rootless and homeless.

"In Israel I can write my articles and books. There is a democracy, but one day I will find myself without a home and a land. Hussein will put me in jail — for five years, ten years — but when I come out I will return to my home. I don't want an occupation, any occupation, but today I prefer Hussein to the Israelis!"

He knows what he is talking about. When Hussein ruled the West Bank, Abu-Shilbaye was imprisoned for five years because of a newspaper article he wrote. He never accepted the Israeli occupation, but, in the early years, he freely admitted that it was better than a Jordanian one.

A stout, smiling, gray-haired man, Abu-Shilbaye lives near Wadi Joz in Arab Jerusalem. In his cool house one always gets a cup of strong, black coffee, a bowl of fruit, and plentiful offers of the cigarettes he himself chain-smokes. He has always said that the PLO is the rightful representative of the Palestinians, and he has always been prepared to say aloud what others prefer to say off the record: there must be mutual recognition between Israelis and Palestinians. Israel is here to stay, but there can be no peace without a free Palestinian state. He has written a number of books and numerous articles and pamphlets on the subject.

Abu-Shilbaye used to live in what is now the Israeli coastal plain. He owned land near Lydda and some orange groves in what is now the luxury neighborhood of Savyon. "I should be a millionnaire." He laughs, but he speaks seriously when he says he is prepared to relinquish his claim on his former land. He sincerely believes that both sides have to recognize current realities.

In 1948 he fled to Syria, where he was among the founders of the Arab Socialist *Ba'ath* party. The Ba'ath rules Syria to this day, but it has been corrupted into an instrument of President Hafez Assad's military rule. Abu-Shilbaye came to East Jerusalem in 1954 and was soon imprisoned. Returning after five years, he became a schoolmaster, still writing, but steering clear of political subjects. During this period he translated Edgar Snow's *Red Star Over China* into Arabic.

When the Israelis took over, Abu-Shilbaye took advantage of his new-found freedom to write for the East Jerusalem Arabic daily *El-Kuds*, calling for an independent Palestinian state to be set up in the West Bank and Gaza, with East Jerusalem as its capital. But his freedom was not unlimited. His application to be allowed to form a political party was turned down by the Labor government.

Abu-Shilbaye admits that part of the problem is that the Palestinians have not secured independence from the Arab regimes. Each PLO faction, he says, is aligned with a different Arab state. The faction leaders represent the interests of Syria, Iraq, and Libya, and not the interests of the Palestinians. A PLO moderate, Issam Sartawi, was a victim of inter-Arab rivalry when he was gunned down in Portugal, he notes.

When Sadat came to Jerusalem, Abu-Shilbaye published an open letter to Yasir Arafat, pleading with him to join the Egyptian president and thus "challenge Begin with something other than armed conflict."

On a visit to the United States, Abu-Shilbaye met Dr. Walid Khalidi, one of the most eloquent Palestinian spokesmen in that country. "I told him that the Palestinians were walking in the wrong direction," said Abu-Shilbaye. "He agreed with me and said he had already told PLO leaders so."

The Palestinians had lost a great chance by rejecting the Sadat initiative. "If Arafat, Hussein, and Assad had come to Jerusalem with Sadat we would be facing a different situation today," he asserted. People were afraid to talk aloud, he noted, but off the record most Arabs admitted that Sadat had been right.

I asked Abu-Shilbaye about a dialogue between Israel and local West Bank leaders, and he shook his head sadly. "We are too weak," he opined. "We are like the branches of a tree. There are two trunks: the PLO and Hussein." He thought that as many as 80 percent of the West Bankers supported the PLO. The other 20 percent, mainly the rich landowners, supported Hussein.

He talked enthusiastically about the past, when many of the leading writers, poets, and physicians in the Muslim world had been Jews. The Arab-Israel clash was the first time the two peoples had been enemies, he contended.

"I do not hate the Jews," he told me. "I am afraid of them, but that is different. There is a will for peace."

However, he insisted that there could not be Jewish settlements in a Palestinian state. Jews could live there, but the first law that should be passed should prohibit Jews from buying land; "Otherwise, you will buy us out."

"The Arabs are not short of money," I suggested.

"Oh, they have money," he said contemptuously. "They have money for casinos and girls. I know my people. They are weak; they will sell their souls for money; but when we have our own land it will be different."

Jewish settlement in the West Bank is also the main worry of Bethlehem Mayor Elias Frej. "*Habibi*, last week your defense minister was in Etzion [south of Jerusalem] and he told the radio that there will be thousands of settlements with hundreds of thousands of settlers," he pointed out. "When Israel succeeds in doing this, what will be left for us? We will be a people without land — landless, powerless, stateless people. What are the West Bank Arabs worth without land?"

I spoke to Frej in his office above Manger Square, across from the Church of the Nativity. Bethlehem is prosperous. Its shops and cafés are full of tourists and pilgrims. A great deal of construction goes on. The atmosphere in the town is more relaxed than anywhere in the West Bank except Jericho. The IDF is not much in evidence. Driving north from Hebron, I always heave a sigh of relief when I reach Bethlehem.

The mayor of Bethlehem is short and stocky. His pear-shaped face, with its bright, black eyes and black mustache, is lively and expressive. His voice is low and soft, but occasionally it takes on a tone of near despair.

His newly built municipal office is light and comfortable. His secretary, in jeans and a sleeveless blouse, the only female municipal employee in the West Bank, brings us coffee and freshly squeezed orange juice.

The Christian mayor of a Christian town, Frej has proved himself an adept survivor, good at dodging through the raindrops. As the only "moderate" mayor to be elected in the 1976 landslide, he has somehow contrived to keep his bridges open to the Israelis, the Jordanians, the PLO, the West Bank nationalists, and the United States. He does not represent many outside his Christian enclave of Bethlehem, and he could never be a candidate for leadership of a Palestinian state, but his is one of the shrewdest minds in the West Bank. Given the right circumstances, he could play a vital behind-the-scenes role.

"The Israeli bulldozers are working and the Arabs are chattering," he told me. "Gilo [a Jewish suburb near Bethlehem] is bigger than Bethlehem itself. In Kiryat Arba you will soon have Jewish boys who have never known Israel without the West Bank going into the army."

Despite his pessimism, Frej feels there is still a chance for a reasonable settlement, but once the Jewish population of the West Bank passes one hundred thousand, "What Israeli government is going to ask them to leave — even for the sake of peace?"

He says that he knows his views are not popular in the West Bank, but he is not looking for applause. "We Palestinians have been missing the train since 1947," he said. "We let the train go by and then we say we want a more comfortable train."

He had pleaded with his fellow mayors, he told me, not to boycott the civil administration. The municipalities were all that the West Bankers had left. "Is it better to have Israeli army officers running Nablus and Ramallah?" he demanded.

The Israeli government did not want peace with the Palestinians, he said. It wanted to colonize the land. It believed that the West Bank was part of the Land of Israel and that "might is right." Frej had no time for the "village league" people, dismissing them scornfully as "a bunch of illiterates." Anyway, he pointed out, if the government had been serious about the leagues it would not have dismissed Muhammad Naser when he wanted to establish his political party.

The Lebanon war, thought Frej, had been a defeat for Israel. From Israel's point of view it had been ridiculous to sign a peace treaty with Lebanon. When had there been a war between Israel and Lebanon? But the Lebanese had been right to sign. They were right to try to secure an Israeli withdrawal. As for those Arab regimes which were against the treaty, "Let them come and throw the Israeli army out of Lebanon — if they can."

The Lebanese had secured a good settlement; the Israelis had not. Before the Lebanon war there had been hundreds of IDF soldiers patrolling in Lebanon — albeit unofficially; under the new agreement they would have fifty.

"Three Israeli soldiers in a jeep with three Lebanese soldiers." He laughed. "Did Israel go to war for that?"

Frej had supported the Sadat peace initiative; now he supported the Reagan initiative. One gets the impression that he will support any initiative, because anything is better than the fluid status quo, with Israeli settlement increasing every day.

The important thing was to move forward, he stressed. Anything that decreased Israeli control and gave the Palestinians progress toward self-rule was good, he said. Any scheme that would stop Jewish settlement and get rid of the so-called civil administration was to be supported.

"Let us begin with an autonomous entity, which would enable us to administer ourselves," he suggested. The entity would not need an army, he said. The combined Arab armies had not defeated Israel, so what was the point of a Palestinian army? He was in favor of open borders between a Palestinian entity and Israel; the seventy thousand West Bank workers who earned their living in the Jewish state should continue to do so.

The question of the Jewish settlements should be negotiated. The Etzion bloc had been Jewish before 1948, so that was settled. On the other hand, Kiryat Arba, the Jewish suburb of Hebron, was a notable problem. The whole matter had to be negotiated "with cool heads." The important thing was to start the process. "If we remain aloof, weak, and divided, the Jews are going to get everything!"

Frej published, in the *Washington Post*, an op-ed article calling for a PLO plan to challenge the Israelis to peace. He stated that it should be a Palestinian plan rather than an Arab plan, and it had to convince the Jews. Even the most extreme people in the West Bank said privately that there was no alternative to recognizing Israel, so why not proclaim it publicly?

"After Sabra and Shatila, while everyone was still crying, I called for a Palestinian peace plan, which would embarrass Begin and Sharon. I told the PLO it is no good refusing to recognize the Israelis, refusing even to appear on a joint television program with them. I told them that Peace Now is fighting our battle, but we are not brave enough to join hands with them."

Nowhere on the West Bank is the situation more extreme than in Hebron, where militant Jewish settlers live cheek by jowl (literally) with fundamentalist Muslim Arabs.

Enter the apartment of Rachel Nir, adjoining the Avraham Avinu Synagogue in the former Jewish quarter of the town. Go into the guest bedroom and open the barred shutters on the window. You will be able to reach down and steal a candy from the tray on the head of an Arab vendor in the Casbah market below: that is how close together Jews and Arabs live in the city of the Patriarchs.

Rachel, a beautiful Yemenite in her thirties, with a kerchief covering her head and a smile of extraordinary sweetness, explains that she used to live in Shave Shomron, a new Gush Emunim settlement in the northern part of the West Bank, but she and her husband, an electronics engineer, decided that they did not like living behind the barbed-wire security fence that surrounded the village.

"That is no way to live in the Land of Israel," she told me. "We have to live naturally, among the people."

An Israeli soldier stands guard in front of Avraham Avinu, but Rachel and her young children go shopping in the winding lanes of the Casbah unescorted.

Abraham, the first Jew, bought the Machpela Cave in Hebron in which to bury his wife, Sarah, some four millennia ago. The Muslims also revere Abraham's memory, and they call the cave the Ibrahimi Mosque.

The modern Jewish presence in Hebron predates Zionism by several hundred years. The Avraham Avinu Synagogue and the surrounding Jewish neighborhood were built in the sixteenth century, and Jews continued to live there until the 1920s. In 1929 there were anti-Zionist riots, and fifty-nine Jews were killed in a pogrom. The survivors were evacuated, and no Jews lived in Hebron until the area again came under Jewish control after the Six Day War.

In 1968 Rabbi Moshe Levinger led a party of Jews in a six-month sit-in at Hebron's Park Hotel. The group subsequently stayed, for four years, in the compound of the military government headquarters in the town. Their persistence paid off and the Labor government of Golda Meir established Kiryat Arba, now a modern Jewish suburb overlooking the Arab town. But his success did not satisfy the redoubtable rabbi.

In 1981 it was his American-born wife, Miriam, who took the initiative. She led a sit-in by a dozen women at the Hadassah Building, a former Jewish property, in the center of town. She wrote to Ezer Weizman, then defense minister, that King David had appeared to her in a dream and ordered her to restore a Jewish presence in Hebron.

At first the Begin government balked at the idea, but once again the single-minded obstinacy of the settlers prevailed, and the government is planning and carrying out the reconstruction of Hebron's former Jewish neighborhood.

Jews live in a number of houses in downtown Hebron. Bet Romano, adjoining the Arab market, is now the site of a yeshiva, and several Jewish families live on the top floor over the college. It was there that I met Neura Bleicher, wife of the rabbi who heads the yeshiva.

Dressed in the long skirt and long-sleeved blouse of the Orthodox, the thirty-one-year-old Neura dandled two of her five children on her knee as we talked. "I left a beautiful villa, set among lawns, to come here," she said, pointing to the dingy, high-ceilinged room, its walls stained with damp. "I was reluctant to come, and now I am here I merely wonder why I didn't do it sooner."

When she had visited Hebron, she had been scared stiff, she admitted, but now that she lived here, she was not in the least afraid. "Do you know why?" she asked. "Because I am the owner, the proprietor. It belongs to me Don't say that we want to throw the Arabs out; that is a libel. They can live here with full rights, but *I* will grant them those rights because it is *my* town!"

Neura Bleicher sees nothing strange in twenty-odd Jewish families claiming ownership over a town of seventy thousand Arabs. Every people has its own homeland, she declares, and the Land of Israel is the home of the Jewish people.

"I am not harming anyone by living here; I am benefiting the entire world. The Jewish people is the heart of humanity and if the heart is healthy, the body will be healthy. If the people of Israel is healthy, the whole world will be healthy. And the people of Israel will only be healthy when it is standing upright in its own land."

If Hebron has attracted the most extreme among the Jewish West Bank settlers, they are matched by the Arab inhabitants of the town. Hebron has no theaters, no cinemas, no bars or other places of entertainment, but there are plenty of mosques. In Hebron, the irresistible force of Jewish Messianism has come up against the immovable object of Muslim fundamentalism. This, along with the close physical proximity of the two communities, is a formula for disaster.

The cycle of violence in recent years has included the gunning down of five Jewish settlers who were returning from prayer; random shooting at Arab houses; the placing of a booby-trapped explosive device outside a mosque; the knifing to death of a Jewish yeshiva student in broad daylight in the market and the setting alight of the market in revenge; and an armed attack by three masked men on the town's Islamic College, in which three Arab students were killed and thirty-three injured. Nowhere is Arab terrorism more ruthless or Jewish vigilantism more extreme.

The Machpela Cave, both synagogue and mosque, is a focus of friction. There have been numerous brawls between worshipers, and scrolls of both the Torah and the Koran have at different times been mutilated.

"I am prepared to have Jews returning to Hebron," declares former mayor Mustafa Natshe, "but not Rabbi Levinger and his fanatical followers."

Natshe, a soft-spoken chemical engineer of fifty-three, was the acting Arab mayor until the military authorities dismissed him in July 1983 after the stabbing of the yeshiva student, accusing him of incitement. Receiving me in his comfortable drawing room, over the inevitable cup of strong black coffee, Natshe admitted that he had encouraged Arab market vendors and bus drivers to resist eviction to make way for more Jewish settlement, but he insisted that he has always used legal means, like applying to the Israeli supreme court. He denied ever having advocated violence.

The only way he could envisage Jews living in Hebron, he said, was within the context of a comprehensive solution of the Palestinian problem. There must be an independent Palestinian state alongside Israel. Palestinian refugees must be allowed to return

from all over the world. Those who had lived in what was today
Israel must be offered the alternative of compensation or return.
"In the present situation," he told me, "everything is a problem,
but with peace, anything is possible."

If there were peace, a Jew might prefer to live in Hebron (in
Palestine) and an Arab to live in Israel, said Natshe. His father
had owned land in what was now Ramat Hasharon, a prosperous
suburb of Tel Aviv. Maybe he would live there. He smiled.

Unlike Frej or Abu-Shilbaye, Mustafa Natshe will not criticize
PLO policy. The Camp David formula did not go far enough, he
maintains, but if Israel were to recognize the legitimate rights of
the Palestinians, the PLO would surely recognize Israel.

What if Israel were to take this step and the PLO did not
respond? Natshe shrugs and smiles. That is inconceivable, he
says.

If the majority of the Palestinian refugees elected to return to
Israel, it could be a serious obstacle to the peace process, but I
do not think that a majority would. Many live in the United States,
Canada, and South America, and they would stay put. Even those
who live nearer — in Lebanon, for example — would, for the most
part, be prepared to settle down where they are.

Six months into the war, in November 1982, I spent two days
in the ruins of the Palestinian refugee camp of En Hilwe and
spoke with a number of Palestinians. Most of the young men
were in detention at the Ansar camp, but a number were still
around.

Hallil, a teacher, dapperly dressed in tweed jacket and gray
trousers, told me that he would not start rebuilding his destroyed
home until the situation became clearer.

What did he want to do? He thought carefully before replying
that the best thing would be to return home to "Palestine." He
was speaking of his former home near Haifa in what is now Israel.
All the refugees would like to go back, he said, if they had a free
choice.

No, he admitted in answer to my next question, he did not think it was a realistic idea. He would be prepared to remain in Lebanon — his second choice — if the local Lebanese accepted him and he could live there safely. He would like to become a citizen of Lebanon and settle down. En Hilwe would be fine if it were rebuilt properly as a decent neighborhood. It had become his home.

Not so Issam, whose parents had been killed in the war. He had interrupted his civil engineering studies in the United States when he heard of his parents' death. He was remarkably free of bitterness. He would consider living in Israel, he told me. He had heard it was a modern country. It might be a good idea to get a job in one of the Gulf states — you could make good money there. But he was not sure he wanted to live in an Arab country at all. First, he wished to return to the United States to complete his studies and he might stay there. He had a girlfriend in Texas, an American girl, and he felt quite American.

Many others spoke in a similar vein, and most of them, like Hallil, envisaged remaining in Lebanon. The refugee problem will be a big one when it comes to solving the Israel-Arab conflict, but not, I think, insurmountable. Many Israelis argue that there is simply not enough room in Israel and the West Bank. I wonder if those same people believe that there is enough room to absorb twelve million Jews. I am confident that they do.

It is absolutely impossible to know which Palestinian leaders could seize the leadership of their cause and negotiate with Israel on the basis of mutual recognition. A poll, taken during the fight between Yasir Arafat and his rivals in the PLO in Lebanon in 1983, showed 90 percent of West Bankers for Arafat. Although he has not really moved to a moderate stance, he is widely perceived as moderate and therefore the West Bank poll represents a vote for moderation. I am confident that Frej is right when he says that "even the most extreme people in the West Bank" are ready to recognize Israel.

If a new Israeli administration adopted a dynamic, forward-looking policy of compromise and mutual recognition, it would lead to a response on the Palestinian side, but let us leave the last words in this chapter to a West Bank journalist, Jamil Hamad. In an article in the *Jerusalem Post*, he wrote about the 1983 battles in Lebanon's Bekaa Valley between rival sectors of the PLO:

"Perhaps because the Palestinians here [in the West Bank and Gaza] are not situated in the Bekaa, we are in exactly the right position from which we can send a message to Damascus and Tripoli, a message that we are tired of Arab interference in Palestinian affairs. We are tired of officers who drive tanks and shoot guns just to hold on to their own power. We are sick of the Arab world determining what we want the PLO to do for us. It is not the business of any Arab country to involve itself in our affairs. The time has come for the Palestinians to create their own hope."

5
The Way Out

"Men and nations sometimes behave wisely once they have exhausted all the other alternatives."

This witty comment was made by Abba Eban. If anything illustrates how Israel has changed, how our standards have dropped, how "this is not the Israel we have seen in the past," it is the eclipse of the urbane, intelligent Eban.

What is worth remembering is that it was his intellectualism that appealed to the public — not least among the Edot, who revere learning, as all Jews do. Eban was Israel's eloquent representative at the United Nations, but he was also Labor's most popular speaker in the deprived neighborhoods and development towns. It should also be stressed that Menachem Begin was a fine orator, with a stylish Hebrew, which explains some of his appeal for the Edot; unfortunately, Begin jettisoned his former eloquence and preferred to utter macho threats to the Arabs and scathing denunciations of his Jewish political opponents.

It may be some time before Eban's talents will again be at the disposal of the Israeli nation. Meanwhile, let us use his statement about acting wisely to move forward, for, after the Lebanon war, we have indeed "exhausted all the other alternatives." Wisdom is just about all we have left.

There have been numerous ingenious proposals for solving the

Palestinian (or West Bank) problem, from Begin's proposal for autonomy under Israeli rule to an Israel-Jordan condominium. Official Labor party policy remains territorial compromise with Jordan, based more or less on the Allon plan. Some have suggested what they call functional partition, whereby West Bank Arabs would vote for the Jordanian parliament and find their political self-expression there. There have been suggestions for shared sovereignty, or indefinite "no sovereignty." All these suggestions, which come from the Israeli side, fail to take into consideration that just as the Israelis insisted on having a Jewish state in 1948, so in 1983 did the Palestinians want a Palestinian state.

We must not allow ourselves to be panicked into the belief that the options have been closed. They have not. Arabs still outnumber Jews in the West Bank by thirty to one. Furthermore, in poll after poll, at least half the Israeli people express themselves in favor of territorial compromise — this in the absence of a credible Arab or Palestinian proposal and a situation in which the Palestine Liberation Organization, "the sole legitimate representative of the Palestinians," still officially hews to a policy of destroying Israel by armed struggle.

Those Israelis who believe that all the Land of Israel must remain with the Jews as their eternal inheritance will not agree to a compromise. Nor will those who believe that the Arabs are irredeemably hostile to Jewish nationhood and are simply awaiting their chance to destroy Israel. According to these people, even the Egyptians are just trying to destroy us by subtler means. They will not be persuaded otherwise. Even when Egypt retained diplomatic relations with us throughout the Lebanon war, recalling its ambassador only after Sabra and Shatila, they were not convinced.

Most Israelis, however, are not extremists. Most are not convinced that our fate is one of endless war and conflict. The Lebanon war showed the futility of the military way, and the lesson is beginning to sink in.

The majority of Israelis are still deeply suspicious; it would be impossible to get an Israeli majority for a Palestinian state. A formula that will convince the Palestinians that their state is on the way, without alarming the Israeli majority, must be devised.

The Palestinians will not only have to accept the absence of their own army. They will have to accept the presence of the Israeli army for a considerable time. Above all, they will have to accept delay in the implementation of their statehood.

In 1978 the Israeli Knesset voted by an overwhelming majority to approve the Camp David accords and the Israel-Egypt Peace Treaty. Faced with the prospect of giving up energy self-sufficiency and the strategic depth of Sinai for a "piece of paper," the Knesset took the risk.

The time has come to mobilize this majority once more, in favor of the second part of the Camp David accords, the Framework for Peace in the Middle East, which was also signed by Anwar Sadat, Menachem Begin, and Jimmy Carter at the end of the Camp David summit. The framework offers a flexible formula for putting the Palestinians on the road to self-government while safeguarding Israel's security.

The framework determines that "Egypt, Israel, Jordan, and the representatives of the Palestinian people will negotiate a solution of the Palestinian problem in all its aspects." It envisions a five-year transition period in the West Bank and Gaza, during which Israeli military government would be withdrawn and replaced by an autonomous authority "elected by the inhabitants of these areas." Israel, Egypt, and Jordan were to agree on "the modalities" for establishing this autonomous authority.

The Israel Defense Forces were to be deployed in certain areas, but internal security would be gradually transferred to a "strong local police force." Israel and Jordan were to carry out joint patrols.

During the five-year transition period — specifically, not later than the third year — Egypt, Israel, Jordan, and "the elected

representatives of the West Bank and Gaza" would start negotiating the final status of these territories.

Begin made it clear at Camp David that Israel reserved the
right to claim sovereignty over the West Bank and Gaza at the
end of the transition period, but the framework spoke of "negotiating the location of boundaries and other security arrange-
ments." It was further specified that a settlement must "recognize
the legitimate rights of the Palestinian people and their just
requirements."

In Begin's view, resolution of the Palestinian problem in all its
aspects and the legitimate rights of the Palestinian people would
be adequately covered by the implementation of full autonomy.
This would give the West Bank and Gaza Arabs self-administration,
but they would not be permitted to legislate, and control of security, land, and water would be in Israeli hands.

The framework does not mention either Jewish settlements or
Jerusalem, which made it unacceptable to the Arab states, except
for Egypt. If the Arab side had reacted favorably to Camp David,
and the Jordanians had joined the process, things might have
been very different.

Israel's government has been only too happy to stall over autonomy while building as many settlements as it can, but it has
been assisted and encouraged by the intransigence of the Arab
side. The slow, tortuous, futile negotiations between Israel and
Egypt were entirely frozen in the light of the Lebanon war.

In September 1982, the day the PLO was ousted from Beirut,
the U.S. administration launched a drive to get the Camp David
accords back on track. Most of the Arab world gave some grudging encouragement to what has come to be known as the "Reagan
initiative," but Israel turned it down flat.

Had King Hussein joined the peace process, it is possible that
Israel would have found itself under considerable pressure, but, as
in the past, the Arab side — specifically the PLO — came to the rescue of Begin's government. After weeks of dithering, Yasir Arafat
turned down the proposal that Hussein represent the Palestinians.

Israel claims that the Reagan initiative is inconsistent with Camp David; Jimmy Carter says it is fully consistent with it. Semantics aside, the initiative goes beyond the framework in a number of fields. It says that East Jerusalem residents should vote for the West Bank and Gaza Authority. It says that there should be "progressive Palestinian responsibility for internal security, based on ability and performance." It calls for a freeze on Jewish settlement in the West Bank. It says that autonomy means "giving the Palestinians real authority over themselves, the land, and its resources, subject to fair safeguards on water." It opposes the extension of Israeli sovereignty over the West Bank and Gaza.

Thus far, the initiative is designed to appeal to the Arab side, but it also specifically opposes the establishment of an independent Palestinian state. Israel contends that the proposals would inevitably lead to a Palestinian state.

This is obviously correct and it would be more honest to say so. A majority could be mobilized in Israel for starting the process along the lines of the Reagan initiative, given two conditions: one, the Palestinian state must be delayed for several years; two, the process must have built-in safeguards, giving Israel the right of veto if its security is threatened.

While a majority of Israelis are sincerely concerned that a Palestinian state would threaten their security, most would be only too pleased to get rid of the West Bank. Many are worried about the deterioration of standards, the drift toward a "South African situation"; even more are heartily fed up with long months of military service and the constant tensions involved in hanging on to the territories.

More and more soldiers refused to serve in Lebanon and the call to bring the boys home rang ever louder. It is only a question of time before a similar situation develops with regard to the West Bank.

No less important is the economic burden of the territories. As the economic situation deteriorates, the willingness of Israelis to invest in the West Bank settlements is declining. When most people were fairly well off, they did not ask too many questions; but as more cuts are made in the standard of living, more people are beginning to resent the money being poured into Judea and Samaria. This factor could be crucial in determining attitudes.

The nationalists realize this, and government supporters are stressing the need to be economically independent. Yigael Hurvitz, Begin's second finance minister, and a fervent exponent of "Greater Israel," has said that it may be necessary to slow down settlement activity in order to save the economy. He is prepared — temporarily at least — to accept Labor's settlement policy, in order to entice them into a government of national unity to tackle Israel's deteriorating balance of payments crisis. Ultimately we may discover that Israel simply cannot afford the West Bank.

The mood in the country is changing. Whereas after the wars of 1967 and 1973 the ferment in Israel was of a nationalist or Messianic character, which led to the emergence of the Land of Israel movement and Gush Emunim, the Lebanon war reversed this tendency. All the protest movements and pressure groups are pushing for peace and compromise.

The revival of Peace Now, the emergence of Netivot Shalom, the dovish religious movement, and the development of such groups as Yesh Gvul, Soldiers against Silence and Parents against Silence, are all significant. The establishment of *Hamizrach Leshalom*, "East for Peace," could yet be the most important of all, because this movement comes from the Edot, one of the strongest parts of the Begin constituency. If the religious front crumbles and the Edot front crumbles, the Begin government consensus could be in deep trouble and the chance for a moderate consensus greater than at any time since 1967.

East for Peace was formed by a group of intellectuals from among the Edot in order to counter the image of oriental Jews as violent, extremist haters of Arabs who are opposed to peace. They have already elicited an amazing response in the poorer neighborhoods and development towns.

An authentic grassroots movement, it aspires to be a great deal

more than just an "oriental Peace Now." Its members aim at a
revolution in Israeli society and attitudes. The Zionist pioneers
from Eastern Europe had little knowledge of either the Arab-
Muslim world or the oriental Jewish world and they have screwed
up their relationships with both, say the leaders of the movement.

"Israel has been facing west too long," declares Shelley Elkayam,
one of the movement's founders. "The time has come for a change
of direction." Shelley, an eighth-generation sabra, feels herself
very much an "oriental Jew." She rejects the term Edot Hamizrach, communities of the East. A community is a small unit,
she says, whereas oriental Jews are in the majority. She defines
people born in Israel as orientals, because Israel is "part of the
East."

Attractive, articulate, outspoken, with a marked impatience for
bullshit, the poetess and former kibbutznik believes that the cultural center of the country has swung east. There is too much
concentration on the kibbutzim and the old centers, she maintains; the poor neighborhoods and the development towns are
"where it's all happening" today. Locations that used to be on
the periphery of Israeli society are becoming central, she says.
Be'er Ya'acov — once a transit camp — is the home of Shlomo
Bar, leader of the *Brera Tivit*, the country's best musical group.
Bar produces "authentic oriental Israeli music," and is a founder-
member of East for Peace. Deputy Prime Minister David Levy
still lives in Bet Shean, a development town in the Jordan Valley,
which is therefore a political center. The Jerusalem slum neighborhood of Musrara has been a center of activity since the days
of the Black Panthers and has produced two Knesset members.
"Things are changing," insists Shelley.

Songwriter Shlomo Bar argues that Israeli music must be Eastern, or Mediterranean, "because we received the Torah on Mount
Sinai and not in Eastern Europe." He maintains that if he manages to create Israeli music which is genuinely oriental, he will
also be able to communicate more directly and more truthfully
with the Arab peoples of the region.

"Judaism is the bridge between East and West," he says. "We are not sitting in the Middle East by accident; we are a sort of rim, or pelvis, connecting the different parts of the world."

Moroccan-born journalist Jules Daniel, who explained how the oriental Jews were maneuvered into becoming hostile to the Arabs, is confident that the new movement will lead to a new feeling of pride in orientalism, akin to the black consciousness movement in the United States. This will result in the jettisoning of the anti-Arab line, because oriental Jews are naturally moderate.

"We don't have this European-style fanaticism," he insists. "Gush Emunim is a foreign import. It has brought European-style nationalism into Judaism. It has no place in the Jewish tradition of Morocco, Yemen, or Iraq."

Daniel notes that it is the poor, mostly oriental Jews who suffer from the diversion of resources to West Bank settlement. Funds that should be used for education, welfare, and building better housing in Israel are squandered to subsidize villa owners in Judea and Samaria. Fortunes are spent on roads and infrastructure. But he stresses that he is just as much opposed to West Bank settlement, "because it will lead to the dispossession of Palestinian Arabs."

East for Peace is dedicated to a just society in Israel, but the justice must also apply to the Arabs — Israeli citizens and West Bankers alike. This is not the first time that oriental Israelis have spoken out about the possibility for reconciliation with the Arabs, but previously such talk was confined to a small group of oriental Jews who lived in Israel before the Zionist immigrants arrived. The important thing about East for Peace is that it has emerged among the immigrants of the 1950s. If it succeeds in becoming a mass movement and making contact with Palestinians and other Arabs, the effects could be far-reaching.

One incident that might point the way the wind is blowing concerns student elections at Haifa University. The student unions have traditionally been political battlefields, with the students identified with Labor-linked or Likud-front groups. Early in 1983 a coalition of oriental Jewish and Israeli Arab students won the election, and they run the student union together.

The significant thing about all these new movements is that they reject both the path of Menachem Begin and the former path of Labor Israel. They want to create something new, something better.

This is in the true tradition of Zionism, which is, above all, a hopeful movement. Real Zionism rejects the idea that it is the perpetual fate of the Jews to fight and struggle. The young sabras of Peace Now, the young Edot Jews of East for Peace, the young religious Jews of Netivot Shalom, and the various soldier dissidents are taking up the Zionist challenge and striking out in new directions. Ultimately, they will assume the leadership of Israel, but they are not yet ready to do so and the gap between them and the political echelon will have to be bridged.

With the utter failure of his militant approach manifest even to him, Menachem Begin resigned. He could not lead Israel out of the blind alley into which he had led it, and his successors show no signs of wanting to. His party could have elected Deputy Prime Minister David Levy to replace him. Although a faithful member of the ruling Likud, Levy would in many ways have been an exciting choice. A representative of the Edot, only forty-five years old, an outspoken critic of Sharon during the Lebanon war, a man who speaks Arabic, Levy might have kept the Likud in power for many years.

Instead the Likud chose the foreign minister, Yitzhak Shamir — an aging reactionary who did not support the Camp David accords and the peace treaty — a pale carbon copy of Begin. Shamir can be expected to lead the country down the same blind alley of extremist fatalism, out of touch with the new ideas and moods developing in Israel. In electing Shamir, the Likud has voluntarily cast itself on the scrap heap of history.

The Labor party, with the protest movements, will have to provide the core of the new leadership, but that party is only marginally more suitable than the Likud to guide this country.

The party leadership is weak and divided, and Labor is still distrusted by the Edot, and it took a flabby lead in opposing the Lebanon war. We should also not forget that it was Labor which started the mistaken policy on the West Bank.

A new, broadly based national leadership, which will strive to create an alternative, rational policy for Israel, must be mobilized from personalities in the existing parties and in the political wilderness. David Levy, rejected by the Likud, will undoubtedly have an important part to play in it.

The pivotal personality is the former president, Yitzhak Navon. He is personally reluctant to enter the political fray and one can understand why, but he is being summoned by history. Navon, who is being talked about as the next leader of the Labor party, can be far more than that. Navon is the man most qualified to lead a new national alliance, which will include the Labor party, the center, some of the Likud, much of the religious camp, and will gain the support of the new protest movements.

In our darkest hour, after the Beirut massacres, it was Navon who had the courage to step out of the presidential ivory tower and call for an investigation by "reliable and independent persons." This special announcement from the presidential office, coupled, it later transpired, with an unprecedented resignation threat, did much to turn the tables in favor of the official inquiry into Sabra and Shatila. On the night of pain and horror, after the murder of peace demonstrator Emile Grunzweig, Navon's televised appeal for moderation and tolerance was the most eloquent and assured.

Like Begin, the benign, white-haired ex-president is a father figure, but unlike Begin, who took to appealing to the lowest common denominator, Navon appeals to our better selves. His message is always one of tolerance and moderation, his tone always civilized and warm. As president he was widely respected and immensely popular. A Labor man, Navon has far wider appeal than his party does. Rather than use his broad appeal for party ends, let him summon the wider constituency to join with him in the new alliance.

A former head of the Knesset Foreign Affairs and Defense Committee, he is an experienced politician. As personal secretary to David Ben-Gurion, he worked under Israel's only statesman to date. The only objection I have heard expressed to his leadership is that he is "too nice a guy." In the new Israel that we must build, this cannot be a disqualification.

Above all, Navon is the man to bring us together after the strident style of the Begin years. Begin polarized the nation in an unprecedented way. He did not invent the resentment of the Edot, but he fanned it. He did not create the enmity of the Arabs, but he delighted in provoking it. The split between religious and nonreligious was always there, but he managed to widen it.

Navon, an oriental Jew born in Israel, has crisscrossed this land and spoken to the ordinary people in their homes and workshops, on their farms, and in their streets. He has found out the simple truth — "We are much better than we think we are."

Speaking Arabic — the same language in which he had communicated with President Sadat — he broadcast a message of sympathy for the victims of Sabra and Shatila to the relatives of the slain, whether Israeli, West Bank, or Lebanese Arabs, from the Arab village of Julis.

Navon will rebuild Israel's severed links with the world and with the Jewish Diaspora, and he will forge links to the Arab world. More than anything else, he will raise the level of public debate and make it more civilized.

Number two on our leadership team is David Levy, Begin's deputy prime minister. Our alliance must be as broad as possible and we need figures from the moderate right, but Levy has earned his place for a number of reasons.

An immigrant to Israel in the 1950s, Moroccan-born, he is a true representative of the Edot. The young leaders of East for Peace make a distinction between those they describe as token orientals — oriental Jewish politicians put on the Knesset or municipal list just because they were from the Edot — and those whom they call authentic oriental leaders, such as Navon and Levy. They note that his political views were more hawkish than theirs, but express the hope of a dialogue with a "man we respect."

Levy earned the respect of wide sections of the population for his moderate stand in the cabinet during the Lebanon war. He was one of the few ministers to stand up to Sharon and the only member of the cabinet who warned of the danger of sending Phalangist forces into Sabra and Shatila.

Tall, broad-shouldered, gray-haired, Levy speaks a trifle ponderously and sometimes seems to be unconsciously imitating Begin, his mentor. But his words are always carefully weighed. He has, on more than one occasion, intervened to solve labor disputes, winning the respect of both labor and management.

Levy has not hidden his deep resentment toward the Labor establishment, speaking out strongly against them in his authorized biography, which has earned him, if anything, more respect.

David Levy represented the government at the funeral of Emile Grunzweig and, in the bitterness and anger of that day, I heard more than one person say that he was the only representative who would have been acceptable. "He is here for the government," remarked one of the mourners, "but I am also under the impression that he is here for himself."

Although Levy has spoken out strongly in favor of West Bank settlement, his actions as housing minister have been less extreme than his words. Indeed, the journal of the West Bank Jewish settlers, *Nekuda*, has accused him of actually implementing the Allon plan. Less than a third of settlement activity is being directed to the heart of the West Bank, maintains *Nekuda*; most of it is in those parts of the West Bank that the Labor opposition wants to retain in the event of territorial compromise with Jordan.

Levy is also among those working for a return to the Likud of former defense minister Ezer Weizman, whose newly moderate views are certainly no secret. Prime Minister Shamir has blocked his return for this very reason. Taking all this into consideration, we may be allowed to conclude that Levy could live with a more moderate policy regarding the administered territories.

Which brings us to the third member of our leadership team: Ezer Weizman, a nationalist who has softened his views, a former Likud leader who is in the political wilderness. The brash, charming Weizman — former Royal Air Force pilot, architect of the superb Israeli air force — was always regarded as a superhawk politically. But where Begin and his comrades had left the mainstream Zionist movement over an earlier partition of the Land of Israel, Weizman is the nephew of Chaim Weizmann, the man who led the Zionist movement on a path of compromise.

Like all Israelis, Weizman was shocked by the Yom Kippur War. He had a very personal reason: his son, Shaul, was gravely wounded in it. It seems to have given Weizman stronger feelings about the cost of conflict.

He was the only Likud leader to support the 1975 Sinai disengagement agreements negotiated by Henry Kissinger, and when Sadat came to Jerusalem Ezer Weizman was the person he liked best. The two men hit it off on a personal level — Weizman is amusing and witty; Sadat had a wonderful sense of humor. More important, the two men shared a sense of history.

As the peace process developed, Weizman was the only Israeli political leader who understood the almost cosmic significance of what Sadat had done. Time after time, "Ezra" (Sadat had difficulty with his name) was sent to pull the chestnuts out of the fire when the negotiations foundered.

Criticized by cabinet colleagues for taking his wife and son along to talks in Egypt and thereby being "too friendly," he exploded: "That is my way of doing things. My way is the way of friendship. If you don't like it, send someone else."

Almost alone in the leadership, Weizman refused to bemoan the handing back of Sinai, to cry about the "sacrifice." Sometimes, he pointed out, you have to uproot something in order to plant something else. Weizman is a big man with a generous, warm personality. He has no patience for the petty, carping, and mean-minded. Some of his new political attitudes are pithily conveyed in his book about the events leading up to the Israel-Egypt treaty, *The Battle for Peace.*

"The chairs around [Begin's] cabinet table," he writes, "were occupied by men who had built their careers on Israel's isolation from the Arab world. There were some you could wake in the middle of the night and with their eyes still closed they could reel off the minutest detail of events in Plonsk in 1910 — but they had not the slightest inkling of what went on in an Arab village within Israel last week."

He is scathing about the tortuous progress of the cabinet toward the 1978 agreement and was furious when Ariel Sharon, then minister of agriculture, established fake settlements in Sinai, which he thought would make bargaining counters. "Israelis from the extremist fringes," he writes, "were constantly lurking in ambush to discredit the peace process."

He never believed, he emphasizes, in the dismal refrain that "the whole world is against us." The true danger, in his opinion, came from those who refused to believe in peace. "When the peace train chugged into the station," he writes in one striking passage, "it found most of the cabinet ministers in an exhausted sleep in the waiting room . . . Peace was a couple of sizes too big for some of them."

He admits that he would like to see Judea and Samaria incorporated into the State of Israel, but he acknowledges that the clock cannot be turned back. "With our army to back us we can afford to be bold and daring in plunging into peace . . . In peace, no less than in war, we must be prepared to take risks," he states. And, in another passage, "We must wage peace as imaginatively as we waged war . . . We have to take peace by storm."

Weizman's pragmatism emerges in his attitude toward confiscation of land in the West Bank, which he opposes because "the most important component of our security is the feasibility of peaceful relations with the Palestinians and the rest of the region. Our future depends on it."

Noting that the population of the Promised Land includes Arabs, "who also view it as their own country," he says he is prepared to accept the fact that "the Land of Israel — Palestine — be partitioned along lines that do not coincide with its historical or geographical boundaries. I do not regard this as a catastrophe . . . Its borders have always fluctuated according to changing political circumstances."

Weizman, the quintessential sabra, his tough pragmatism enhanced by a breadth of vision and a sense of history, is the ideal complement to the wise Navon and the solid Levy. He will add a touch of sparkle to the team, a pinch of leaven.

In forming our team, we must not ignore the religious sector of Israeli society. The non-Zionist Agudat Yisrael can be brought into the alliance simply in the interest of making it as broad as possible. It may be necessary to make some religious concessions and grant some funds to their yeshivot, but we can hope that the breadth of the coalition formed will prevent them from having real power. The religious Zionists, on the other hand, must be brought in as full partners.

Traditionally the coalition ally of Labor, the politically moderate National Religious party was won over by Gush Emunim, which made it the natural ally for the Likud. Zvulon Hammer, the young party leader who led the religious Zionists into Gush Emunim, is the one to lead them out again. He is the fourth member of our leadership team.

Although he was a founder of Gush Emunim, the stocky, forty-six-year-old dark-haired sabra with the knitted skullcap always retained the grudging respect of Israeli doves for his patent sincerity. There was considerable concern when he took over the education ministry, but most of my nonreligious teacher-friends admit that he is a good minister.

Hammer has been having second thoughts about his nationalist credo. His was one of the strongest voices in the cabinet to demand a full inquiry into Sabra and Shatila. "I say that I will not remain a cabinet member if the matter is not properly investigated," he declared at an open meeting of his party. He added, "I have feared for some time during this war at the likely dulling of sensibility to human lives."

In a television interview Hammer referred to the "rights of the Palestinians" and expressed his concern that veneration for the Land of Israel could harm Israel's interests and the spirit of Judaism, "if it is not balanced by other fundamental Jewish values." The right of Jews to settle in the land, he asserted, did not mean their right to "dominate another people."

This interview so infuriated Gush Emunim that Hammer's forthcoming visit to some of their settlements was abruptly canceled. Rabbi Levinger called on him to resign his cabinet seat.

In a later interview with the *Jerusalem Post*, Hammer declared, "I hope the awareness of the limitations of our power will become more widespread. We always have to think of the human and moral price when we send the army to war . . . What happened has aroused basic questions about how Jews use military force." The Lebanon war, he suggested, had brought about a "more balanced approach to realities."

Hammer's combination of sincerity, questioning, learning, and skillful political leadership will be a notable asset to our leadership team and will line up the religious Zionist moderates behind it.

For the fifth member of our team I again look to the political wilderness, but whereas Weizman is an exile from the Likud, Lova Eliav is an exile from Labor. A man on the left of Israel's political scene, one who has held many talks with moderate PLO leaders in Europe, Eliav is nevertheless widely respected, in the country as a whole, by all sections of the political spectrum and in all sectors of the population.

Born in Russia and brought to Israel at the age of three, he was serving in the Haganah by the time he was fifteen. In the 1940s he played a major role in smuggling "illegal" immigrants from Europe. When the state was founded, he was a central figure in handling the absorption of the 1950s immigration.

In the mid-1950s, deciding that something better than the haphazard absorption methods was required, he directed Israel's first regional development scheme at Lachish, between Ashkelon and Beersheba. In Lachish he proved not only a careful planner and forceful administrator, but he showed his imagination when he insisted on living on the spot rather than commuting from Tel Aviv. He later did the same in Arad, forcing the planners and architects to live in the middle of the desert, so their plans would be suitable for the environment.

A unique combination of visionary and man of action, Eliav went into politics and became the secretary-general of the ruling Labor party. From this central position of power, with grassroots support all over the country, there was nowhere to go but up. He seemed destined for a cabinet post — he had already served as a deputy minister — but it was not to be.

Almost alone in the period of euphoria after the Six Day War, and the exasperation with the Arab rejection of recognition of Israel at Khartoum, Eliav pleaded with his party colleagues to recognize the justice of the Palestinian cause. An experienced planner, he proved that Israel could fulfill its Zionist mission within its previous boundaries, and he demanded justice for the people of the West Bank and Gaza.

His views brought him into a head-on confrontation with the formidable Golda Meir, and he was forced to resign. He was subsequently a member of several left-wing parties, but the mood in the country was against him and he made no political headway. During this period he worked as a volunteer orderly in a Tel Aviv hospital. He also maintained contact with moderate elements in the PLO.

After a period of teaching at Harvard, he returned to Israel to spend time in the development towns as a volunteer teacher. He spent a year in Or Akiva, in the center of the country, followed by a year in Kiryat Shmona. He told me that his time there was a "love affair between me and one hundred and fifty Moroccan housewives," to whom he taught Hebrew and Zionist history.

At the outset of the Lebanon war he got himself mobilized into the IDF and toured South Lebanon. He drew up a rehabilitation plan for the Palestinian refugee camps, which was provisionally approved by Sharon, but in the end the matter was taken out of his hands and the cabinet appointed a minister to coordinate welfare activities.

Most recently, he has been acting for the government in an attempt to arrange for a prisoner exchange with the PLO, which has prevented his planned return to politics. "I had hoped to spend another year in a development town — this time in the Negev," he told me, "but now I see I can't afford the luxury. The situation is too critical and I feel I must return to political activity."

Formerly a man of the Labor party, but still at odds with its leadership, he would fit naturally into our national alliance. His presence there would be a spur to moderate Palestinians to trust the new leadership team.

Eliav is the visionary of our team, but with his practical experience in planning and development, he would make a concrete contribution. Apart from his experience in Israel, he has in the past led Israeli teams to plan the rehabilitation of areas hit by earthquakes in Iran and Nicaragua. His work was highly praised by their governments.

He has set out his ideas for the future of the Middle East in a number of books and articles. He envisages a confederation of *Isfalur* (Israel-Palestine-Jordan), and he has a clear idea of the practical steps needed to make such a confederation work.

Navon, Levy, Weizman, Hammer, Eliav — these five leaders could form the center of a new national alliance. I believe that they could line up a broad consensus for doing what must be done.

They are not a bunch of extreme doves, representing the far left of the Israeli political spectrum, but a group that represents much of what is best in this country.

It does not matter how it happens — it does not even matter if some of the individuals I have put forward are actually on the team or not. What is vital is that personalities who represent what they represent reach positions of leadership and reforge what I have called the Camp David consensus.

The moderate left and center must stop being on the defensive. The nationalist way has failed, and failed abysmally. The time has come to present the nation with an alternative vision.

Whichever way it is formed, Israel's new government will face formidable tasks. Somehow it must find a way to get out of Lebanon, which is going to be a great deal harder than it was to get in. Bringing the boys home, without permitting the return of the PLO to South Lebanon and the katyushas to Kiryat Shmona, is going to call for some creative and imaginative bargaining with the Syrians.

The government of Menachem Begin squandered the country's physical resources no less than its moral ones. Just as the willingness of the young (and not so young) soldiers to fight and die has been stretched by an unnecessary war, so have the country's financial reserves been stretched to the limit.

The cost of the war in Lebanon has been gigantic. Apart from actual military operations, which in the modern era are almost beyond human imagination, Israel's army is based on the reserve. The number of production days lost to the economy by soldiers being mobilized for more than a year must be staggering.

Taking into consideration the anguish suffered because of the dead and wounded, it may seem insensitive to note that this also costs money in the form of widows' pensions, disability pensions, grants to orphans, rehabilitation, and the like, but here again the cost is formidable.

Apart from the war, the government has been recklessly pouring money into the Jewish settlements in the West Bank and

Gaza and the roads, water lines, and electricity needed for them. Vast sums have been spent to subsidize the settlers in everything from homes to local workshops and factories.

More money has been squandered on artificially holding down the foreign exchange rate, which ensures cheap foreign holidays and cheap imported consumer goods for large numbers of Israelis. While this made the government popular, it depleted the country's foreign exchange reserves to a dangerous level.

Israel, in the past, always managed to repay its debts. Now it is being forced to take short-term loans to repay its long-term debts. The future is being mortgaged to the present.

Begin's government made it more profitable to speculate on the stock exchange than to establish factories, more worthwhile to sell imported foreign goods than to produce, more sensible to wheel and deal than to work. Our agriculture, once our pride and joy, is in a state of near-total collapse.

Government spending has increased, but production and exports have fallen. Somehow this must be reversed and, in fact, everyone knows how: government spending has to be cut.

Yigael Hurvitz, the finance minister who preceded Yoram Aridor, actually managed to lower the standard of living. It was a brave policy, and during Hurvitz's time at the Treasury the balance of trade improved and the foreign currency reserves increased, but he did not manage to lick inflation. Private consumption has risen exponentially and must be cut, but that is not the real problem — the real problem is government spending.

The government of Yitzhak Shamir was forced to come to terms with this reality, and Yoram Aridor, the profligate finance minister, whom Shamir inherited from Begin, had to resign. His successor, Yigal Cohen-Orgad, is taking some of the necessary steps, but even he is not getting at the root of Israel's economic plight.

Government spending will have to be cut drastically. There is no way that Israel can go on spending a million dollars per day to remain in Lebanon, or pouring hard cash into West Bank settlement. Cohen-Orgad owns a home in the West Bank settlement of Ariel. He and Shamir are ideologically incapable of doing what has to be done, and a new government with different political aims must be formed.

Such a government is going to have to carry out some very tough policies. It will have to take the daring step of freezing settlement in the West Bank — for economic as well as political reasons — a step that will be fought tooth and nail by determined nationalist forces, led by Gush Emunim. It will also have to force down the standard of living and cut all government spending to the bone.

I am in favor of compromising over the West Bank and the emergence of a Palestinian state, but I am not under the illusion that this would be easy or without risk. A policy of peace does not mean that we can cut the defense budget — at least not for many years.

Once a moderate and sensible consensus has been reached, Israel will be launched on a relentless struggle to secure its interests. The continued unification of Jerusalem under an Israeli administration, the maintenance of some Jewish settlements in the West Bank, the adjustment of borders, a large IDF presence in the West Bank and Gaza for years to come — all are requirements that will not seem as obvious to the Arab side, or even to the United States, as they do to Israel. A honeymoon with the Arabs and the rest of the world will not begin the day after Shamir resigns, and those of us who wanted this to happen would do well to recognize reality.

The turmoil in the country shows that it cannot unify around an extreme nationalist policy. The people are not prepared for endless sacrifices in order for Israel to be the "policeman of the West" in the Middle East, or to maintain a "Greater Israel."

Israel's disastrous Lebanese adventure has proved that this country is not a "super-power," as Ariel Sharon boasted. His simplistic vision becomes more and more absurd as the complexities of the situation in Lebanon multiply. Israel's military activities must, in the future as in the past, be confined to securing its own interests.

Even the mighty United States has bitten off a great deal more in Lebanon than it can comfortably chew. Lebanon is not Grenada, and a U.S. confrontation with the Soviet Union in the Middle East will benefit no one. More American military involvement in the region will lose Israel the support of its American friends.

Israel used to boast (justifiably) that it did not "demand the sacrifice of a single American soldier." Well, rather more than one U.S. soldier has died in Lebanon, and it is not much use lecturing the Americans that they are in Beirut for "their own interests."

It is unfair to accuse the Israelis of dragging the Americans into Lebanon; but it does not require a great amount of insight to see that, but for Israel's 1982 invasion, the U.S. Marines would never have landed in Beirut.

Most Israelis are no longer convinced that the Lebanon war brought them any real benefits. We should not expect the U.S. to accept the claim that "Israel achieved a great victory for the West in Lebanon."

The Syrians are ruthless and extreme, but they are not Soviet puppets. Furthermore they are pragmatists. The Lebanese problem will have to be skillfully negotiated with them. There is nothing to be gained by espousing the doctrine that war with Syria is "inevitable." Washington and Jerusalem should stop egging each other on toward confrontation and start giving serious consideration to the shape of a wide-ranging settlement with Damascus. The Syrians should be told clearly that the Golan Heights will be on the table in such a negotiation, along with the Lebanese situation.

The people of Israel can and will become unified around a forward-looking policy that leads to peace. The time has come to tempt the Palestinians into a settlement. The framework agreed on at Camp David and the Reagan initiative are both good starting points. If we reverse the trend of recent years and turn aside from the road that led to Beirut, we can start moving along the path to peace with our neighbors and integration in the Middle East.

Israel must stop looking back and stop fighting yesterday's battles. The Jewish state has won its fight to be recognized — that battle was over the day Anwar Sadat's plane touched down at Ben-Gurion Airport. We do not have to throw caution to the winds, but we can try to get rid of our paranoia.

There is so much that is good in Israel: so much idealism, readiness for sacrifice, willingness to give, compassion, optimism, and vision. In recent years it has been suppressed or diverted. Channeled in the right direction by the right leaders, the effervescent vitality, the inventiveness, and the sheer energy of the Israeli people can again make Israel a country of which we can all be proud.

6
Beyond Zionism

On August 3, 1982, about the same time that John Chancellor was telling us in Beirut that this "is not the Israel we have seen in the past," I was traveling with my family to a wedding in the Negev town of Arad.

For me Arad represents the essential Israel: a pioneer town established in the desert wastes. Two decades earlier I had gone with my wife and two young children to participate in the creation of the new community. We had watched it grow from a few isolated asbestos huts into a thriving town of apartment blocks, private villas, schools, libraries, community centers, banks, shops, hotels, sports fields, swimming pools, cinema, and synagogues.

We lived there for nine years, growing with the town, rejoicing in its successes, bemoaning its failures, mourning its tragedies, sharing its joys. We had forged deep and lasting friendships with many, clashed with some, but over all there had been a pervading sense of unity, of progress, of achievement. It was in Arad that we became Israelis and, although we moved to Jerusalem after nine years, a part of us has always remained there in the desert.

Of the four in the car that hot summer day, three were members of the Israel Defense Forces. I had served in two wars and spent a month a year in uniform almost since the day of my arrival in Israel. Etan, aged twenty-four, just back from Lebanon, was trying valiantly to catch up with his studies. My twenty-one-year-old daughter, Ilana, had her uniform with her. After the wedding ceremony, she was going to put it on and hitchhike back to her army base. Only my wife was not an actual IDF soldier, but she, too, had undergone weapons training for the civil guard.

All of us — and all our friends, whom we would see at the wedding — were intimately and personally involved in the fate of our country. For in Israel you can't "cop-out"; it's not that sort of country and we are not that sort of people.

America had to use the television screen to bring the horrors of the Vietnam War to the population. In Israel we don't need television. The radio reports a clash in Lebanon with Israeli wounded. Ten minutes later the helicopter goes over your house on its way to the Hadassah Hospital, and you look at your wife and both of you wonder whether your son is on board that helicopter. The war is in your drawing room, without television.

On that day, however, as we drove past the Bedouin camps and dry wadis to our former home, the war was banished for a few minutes. Each of us was silent with his or her thoughts and memories of the past. And then, as the buildings of Arad — our town in the desert — appeared faintly on the horizon, I felt again the surge of excitement that always accompanied my approach to the community.

The wedding was held, Israeli style, out on the lawn, but an Arad lawn is not like one in New Jersey or London — nor even in Tel Aviv. The lawn itself was planted in soil that had been especially trucked in and spread over the desert rocks. The trees around it were planted in holes gouged out of the flint by pneumatic drills. Irrigated with water brought by pipeline from the distant north, the shady patch of green had been patiently wrested from the red-brown desert.

Oren, the bridegroom, and his elder brother, Allon, had just returned from Lebanon. Their younger brother, Erez, still a conscript, had received special leave for the ceremony. The bride and the groom stood under an improvised *chuppah* (canopy) held up by the two brothers and two friends. The rabbi conducted the ceremony in high good humor, making several joky asides. The atmosphere was jovial and relaxed.

But after the ceremony there was only one topic of conversation: the war. Carmela, an old friend, told us that her son — I remembered him as a skinny twelve-year-old in ragged shorts and sandals — was a company commander in Beirut. She had always had a tendency to dramatize and now she told us, "Ami is a great hero — everybody tells me he is one of the best, but heaven knows if I will ever see him alive again."

Itzik was also just back from Beirut (who wasn't?) after six weeks with a young paratroop battalion. At forty-five, he was beginning to feel a bit past it. His son had just been accepted for pilots' course, a great honor. In an army with many elite units, the pilots are the most elite of all. His wife, Nira, smiled and said that I could guess what she thought about the war. I could. But then she added, "I feel very detached about it, almost as if it was happening to someone else, as if it was not my problem."

Nira, born in Israel, a former kibbutznik and founder of Arad, whose husband was just back from Beirut and whose son was training to be a pilot, felt that it was not her problem.

I knew just how she felt: it is not our country anymore. Our Israel, the Israel that built Arad, had been superseded by another Israel: the Israel of Menachem Begin.

"I have emigrated," Yul, the bridegroom's father, told me later. "I can't live anywhere but Israel and I can't live here now, so I have emigrated. You see me here, but I am really somewhere else."

Virtually no one at that wedding felt that Begin represented him. It was not a matter of hawk or dove, or even of European or oriental. The people of Arad, Israeli-born sabras, or at least educated in Israel, were uncomfortable with Begin's tone of voice.

Ami Bouganim, of the East for Peace movement, told me, on another occasion, "I feel in exile here. I am living in Israel, but I feel as if it is the Diaspora."

Menachem Begin "de-Israelized" Israel. My artist-friend, Mike

Leaf, seriously wounded in the Sinai Campaign, offered the phrase, "the shtetlization of Israel," from the word *shtetl* (East European Jewish township). ·

Israel's finest young playwright, Yehoshua Sobol, has written extensively about the clash between Judaism and Zionism. His play, *A Jewish Soul*, charts the last night in the life of Otto Weininger, a twenty-three-year-old Viennese Jewish philosopher who shot himself in 1903 and spent all night dying.

Weininger, a self-hating Jew, has Zionist friends and he tells them that their dream will probably not succeed. "Zionism and Judaism cannot survive together. Either Zionism will eliminate Judaism, or Judaism will swallow Zionism."

Sobol sees the Gush Emunim style of nationalism as un-Israeli, as an import from the Diaspora. "I think that Judaism is taking over nationalism," he said in a newspaper interview.

Another sensitive observer of the Israeli scene, Ya'acov Hasdai, is in favor of such a takeover. Hasdai, a lieutenant colonel in the reserves, thinks that we have become too Israeli and should return to our Jewish roots.

In his book, *Be'et Barzel* (In a Time of Iron) he argues that the use of force to solve conflicts is an Israeli tradition and contrary to the traditional Jewish way. In a nation fighting for its life, he writes, it was justified, but since 1967 it has lost its self-restraint and control must be re-established.

The traditional Jewish role of the underdog encouraged support for law and order. "Centuries of exile showed our ancestors the dangers of unrestrained force. Our existence was guaranteed when there was law, order, and moral values. Pogroms occurred when naked force was the way. Thus we became a people that valued law and morality."

Up to this point I agree with Hasdai. Where I part company from him is in his view that the founders of Israel, who built the settlements and mobilized the force with which to defend them, "bequeathed us a state built and established on a culture of strength." His appeal is for Israel to turn inward on itself and become "a little more Jewish." I dispute both the analysis and the conclusion.

Hasdai thinks that the Lebanon war was the natural consequence of an Israeli culture of strength. I think it was more the result of the Jewish inferiority complex. The Israeli is open-minded and peace-oriented; the Jew is frightened, suspicious, and inclined to lash out.

The world (and Hasdai) saw the formidable Israeli war machine unleashed on a bunch of comparatively weak terrorists in Lebanon. Israeli's prime minister saw the IDF as the heroic fighters of the Warsaw ghetto and the PLO as "Hitler in his bunker."

Let us look for a moment at the way Menachem Begin (the Jew) and Ezer Weizman (the Israeli) reacted to Anwar Sadat's peace initiative. Begin was suspicious and grudging; Weizman was jubilant and enthusiastic. Begin stressed the sacrifices Israel was being asked to make; Weizman welcomed the challenge of peace. Begin felt that he had given too much at Camp David and at once backpedaled; Weizman was sure he had not given enough and strove to press forward.

Begin is the archetypal Jew: paranoid, suspicious, shrill; Weizman is the pure sabra: brash, self-confident, insolent. Begin is the Jew of the exile; Weizman represents the Israeli, the new Jew.

What is noteworthy is that Begin does not represent today's Diaspora Jew any more than he represents the Israeli. The American or European Jew who has grown up in the post-Holocaust world, buoyed up by the image of a vibrant, independent Jewish state, is far more like his Israeli cousin than he is like Begin. Only those Diaspora Jews of Begin's generation — and those Israeli Jews who have remained psychologically in exile — speak his language. He is not the Jewish Everyman of two millennia; he is that very specific being, the Jew of the era between the Kishinev pogrom and the Nazi Holocaust.

What does it matter? I hear my readers asking that question. Why the futile semantic debate?

It matters because of the conclusion. Hasdai wants Israel to turn in on itself and become a little more Jewish. I want Israel to turn outward, to return to being Israeli.

To the extent that I want the resources that have been devoted to the West Bank redirected to Galilee, the Negev, the development towns, and the poor neighborhoods, I also envisage a turning inward, but I do not want my country to turn into a Middle East ghetto; I want it to reach out to its neighbors and to take its rightful place in the community of nations.

I am not saying that Israel should deny its Jewish roots. There is much that I would preserve from the Jewish tradition, but there is an Israeli tradition as well and I am not about to jettison that either, even though the Israel of Menachem Begin has tried to.

Let us take the Nazi Holocaust. Israel determined that such a thing would never happen again. It brought Adolf Eichmann to trial, built an impressive memorial at Yad Veshem in Jerusalem, which is at once a memorial museum and a research center, and forged a powerful army that struck back at attackers.

For many Israelis the rescue of Israeli hostages at Entebbe in 1976 was the supreme illustration that Jews in trouble anywhere had someone who looked after them, worried about them. It was a moment of pride and relief for the whole nation.

Yitzhak Rabin, then the Israeli prime minister, gave a laconic and factual account in the Knesset when he described his decision. It was almost a military briefing. Not so Menachem Begin, then leader of the opposition. He delivered a dramatic oration describing, almost with relish, the way the Israelis and Jews had been separated from the other hijacked passengers at Entebbe, recalling that individuals had been separated for "life" and "death" at the concentration camps in Nazi Europe.

It was not even an accurate parallel: in the concentration camps, the people were indeed singled out for life and death, but on the basis of whether they could be worked to death as slave laborers or gassed at once. It was not Jew and Gentile the Nazis were separating: they were nearly all Jews.

It would not be an exaggeration to say that Begin wallowed in the Holocaust. He mentioned it in almost every public speech. He lectured the world on its sins against the Jewish people. To this extent I do not find myself condemnatory: the world can do with a certain amount of lecturing on this subject; it is all too readily forgotten.

Where I depart from Begin is in his comparison of the Holocaust to everything else. Entebbe was only one instance. He also compared victims of PLO terror to Holocaust victims and Arafat to Hitler. The Christians of Lebanon, said Begin, were facing a "Holocaust."

The problem with this sort of rhetoric is that it cheapens what was a unique event. There has been nothing like the Nazi Holocaust, either before or since. There were massacres, persecutions, murders, killings, discrimination, hatred, violence. All these things have occurred and still occur in the world today. But there was only one Holocaust.

Where the Israeli reaction was dignified and appropriate, Menachem Begin's was shrill and ultimately self-defeating. He succeeded in making this event of no less than cosmic significance into a bore.

Moshe Dayan used to criticize his prime minister for "muscle-flexing." It was a typical Dayan phrase. He meant that Begin should stop shouting threats at his friends and enemies. Dayan, the sabra, was ready to act. He could be cheeky and abrasive, but he knew when to be more restrained. Nothing illustrates what I am talking about better than the contrasting attitudes of the two men toward Arab terrorism.

Back in the days when he was chief of staff, Dayan visited a kibbutz near the Gaza Strip (then under Egyptian control). One of its members had been murdered and horribly mutilated. At the time there was a feeling of fury in the settlement, but Dayan coolly reminded the kibbutzniks that the Arabs who had done the deed had probably lived on the site of their kibbutz. "You cannot expect them not to feel hatred for us," he remarked.

After a horrible terrorist raid, in which a two-year-old girl had been brutally murdered, Begin reacted differently. Describing the act of murder in lurid detail, he pronounced the murderers to be "two-legged beasts."

Begin managed to dismantle some of the Israel that had grown up in three decades. The fortnightly satirical show, *Nikui Rosh* (Cleaning the Head), was very much an Israeli institution. Its humor was Israeli — not at all Jewish — sharp, biting, corrosively funny. Golda Meir hated it and Begin's nominee for the Israel Broadcasting directorship, Yosef Lapid, simply would not permit it on the air. He claimed that he would allow a satirical show, "if one were submitted," but we all know that this is complete eyewash. Every time a program implies slight criticism of the government, its representatives on the Broadcasting Authority board erupt in anger, and apologies are always hastily delivered.

I realized how much we missed *Nikui Rosh* when I went to see another of the same team's satirical shows, *Yordim al Hashavua* (Making Fun of the Week), which is performed in theaters and halls up and down the country. The show started off by laughing at the demand to settle in the West Bank and eventually to bring it under our sovereignty. A trio sings (in English), parodying a famous American folk song:

> This land is my land,
> This land is . . . *my* land . . .
> This land was made for me and me.

It proceeded to a brilliant impersonation of Ariel Sharon:

Interviewer: What were the main gains of the Lebanon war, Mr. Sharon?

Sharon: Don't be ridiculous. You know very well I can't answer that question. Only *I* know what the gains are and I'm not about to tell you. Haven't you heard of security?

There was a deeply moving poem about a soldier who had not been allowed to grow up because of all the wars he had been in, and the satire occasionally verged on the savage: "Sadat and Begin pledged, 'No more war.' Sadat is no more and Begin went to war."

It is not the gentle, mocking Jewish humor. There is an almost total lack of reverence: humbug is pierced with a sharp, rapierlike wit and also sometimes bonked on the head with a gigantic club. The audience loved it, showing how much had changed in past years. It is unthinkable that such a show could appear every two weeks on national television in Begin's Israel, but it plays to packed houses in theaters and halls.

When Chaim Weizmann, Israel's first president, lay dying, he spoke some final words to his friend and colleague, Meyer Weisgal. "The Jews are a small people, but also a great people. They are an ugly people, but also a beautiful people. They are a people that builds and a people that destroys. They are a people of genius and at the same time a people of enormous stupidity."

These things could, of course, be said of any people, but somehow we Jews and Israelis are a people of extremes: extreme in what we do and extreme in the reactions we provoke. If Sabra and Shatila were a point of shame in our history, the subsequent protest and the Kahan report were reasons for deep pride. Overcondemned for the massacres, we were overpraised for our reaction to them.

No one is neutral about us. I am sure that observers of the war between India and Pakistan found themselves in sympathy with one side or the other. Americans took sides in the Falkland Islands war. In the Persian Gulf war, some back the Iranians and others the Iraqis. But nowhere is the partisanship so shrill, so extreme, as in the Israel-Arab conflict.

Is it our extremism that causes this reaction? Our ability to grate on the nerves of some, while charming others? We are the first to complain if anyone is indifferent. We prefer people to praise us and agree with us. Henry Kissinger once said that "Israelis only regard you as objective when you agree with them one hundred percent." We are happy to enter into zestful arguments with our opponents as well. What really annoys the Israeli is when someone refuses to take sides.

We complain that the world holds us up to impossibly high standards, but no one holds us up to higher standards than we do ourselves. Columnist Yoel Marcus, writing in *Ha'aretz*, compared Israel to a boy he knew at school. Benzi, he recalled, was a terror. He drove his teachers mad and they, for their part, tended to blame him for everything that went wrong.

Israel, suggested Marcus, was like Benzi: a bit guilty, but unfairly assessed. He noted that the Jews had historically been accused of everything from using the blood of Gentile children for Passover matzo to planning to take over the world. Iraq, famous for its public hangings, was able to secure a unanimous demand in the UN Security Council for an "impartial inquiry into the mass poisonings in the West Bank," a charge that was proved entirely spurious.

Yet Marcus concludes, "We are guilty of forgetting that we cannot behave as other peoples. We must try harder to remember Ben-Gurion's command to be a 'light unto the Gentiles.'"

What other people has such arrogance and such humility? I cannot decide whether we are sublime or ridiculous. We are probably both, but, of course, not just a bit one way or the other. We have to be grossly, disgustingly ridiculous and grandly, superbly sublime.

Arthur Koestler once wrote that "Jewry is the human condition carried to its extreme." He came to the conclusion that the Jews should stop being extraordinary because it had cost them too much. The creation of Israel, he thought, was the chance. Now Israel could become a nation like other nations and Jews could make individual decisions: either to become Israelis or to assimilate into their countries of residence. Koestler himself took the second option.

I do not go as far as Koestler. I don't think we can ever be quite like other peoples, but we can become a bit more normal and we should. Hence, we must develop our Israeli personality rather than return to our Jewish persona. It is the Israeli, albeit with his Jewish heritage, who will fit into the Middle East landscape: Ben-Gurion with his open-necked shirt, not Begin with his smart lounge suit.

In practical terms this means a stupendous effort both internally and externally. The effort poured into Jewish settlement in the West Bank cannot be immediately redirected. Much of the energy and resources must eventually be directed toward the poor neighborhoods and the development towns in Israel, to Galilee and the Negev, but for a time the West Bank should continue to receive Israeli assistance for the good of all its inhabitants.

Nor can the defense budget be cut overnight, or the military industries converted into something more constructive. While it faces the practical problems of a changeover, Israel is going to need a strong army and a defense industry for many years. It would be naive to think otherwise.

Ultimately, however, development of our country will proceed simultaneously with that of our neighbors. Israeli agriculture, which has declined in recent years to the point of collapse, will be revived and industry will be fostered.

Utilization of land and water resources will be supplemented by hydroponics and other more advanced methods of intensive cultivation. In recent years Israeli scientists have developed dwarf fruit trees to facilitate harvesting and tomatoes that can be harvested by combine. Such invention will be expanded and increased, helping the hungry world to feed itself.

The greening of the Negev must be carried out without disturbing the desert ecosystem. Once we thought it was enough to bring a waterpipe to the arid soil; now we know more. We must set ourselves to catch up with the ancient Jewish, Nabataean, and Byzantine inhabitants of the Negev, who built their large cities with the support of run-off agriculture.

The run-off method, which conserves water from the natural rainfall and makes use of resources in the desert without bringing in materials from the outside, can develop the area without destroying its essential character. Run-off irrigation can also be used to create parks and gardens.

The industrialization of Galilee must be for the good of its Jewish and Arab citizens alike. Solar and other forms of energy will be improved. The cooperative forms of the kibbutz and moshav will be enhanced and other ways will emerge.

The initial moves toward conciliation with our neighbors will lead to the establishment of a Palestinian state, but withdrawal from the West Bank and Gaza does not mean cutting ourselves off from them. Having agreed on our boundaries, we will strive to make them irrelevant.

Jews and Palestinians will live, trade, and work in the others' countries. Jews will teach Palestinians to be better farmers, more efficient administrators, more inventive industrialists. Palestinians will teach Jews to build cool, beautiful houses, to live in harmony with our surroundings, to relax. Jewish dynamism will be tempered by Palestinian fatalism. Palestinian conservatism will be leavened by Jewish vitality. Jews will become more patient; Palestinians will become less phlegmatic.

The future points toward one world. There can be cultures, ways of life — even religions, but the religion of the future must be to unite, not divide. It must preach tolerance, not intolerance.

Islam, Judaism, and Christianity are all experiencing a revival. A fundamentalism is gaining strength in Iran and much of the Middle East. We see the Messianism of Gush Emunim and the revival of many of the Hasidic sects in Israel. Born-again Christians are increasingly influential in America.

But this is not the wave of the future. It is a reversion, a momentary hiccup in the sweep of history. Religion must be relevant to the modern world, or ultimately fade away. Judaism need not be uncomfortable with this concept. The Jewish religion has developed steadily. The Torah was supplemented by the rest of the Bible. The Bible was amplified by the Mishna, the Mishna was interpreted by the Gemara, and both were explained by the commentaries of the rabbis. Only in our time have the ultra-Orthodox cried, "Stop!"

It will not stop. It will continue: new ways will be found to answer to our spiritual needs and more advanced concepts of morality will be allowed to emerge.

In 1981, during a stint of military service in a small Negev town, I went with a couple of fellow soldiers to see a pornographic movie at the local cinema. It was a revolting display: tasteless, boring, unimaginative — not even erotically exciting. What disgusted us most was the utter lack of merit.

As we walked back to do our guard duty, one of my friends, the grandson of a founder of the Zionist movement, turned to me and said, "When I see a film like that, I am persuaded that the West really is degenerate. I feel some sympathy for Khomeini."

He was wrong. The fundamentalist Muslim revival is no more relevant to the problem than born-again Christianity in the United States or Messianism in Israel. It is an easy way out, not an answer to the challenge of modernism.

I once spent a weekend at the ultra-Orthodox village of Kefar Habad, where members of the Habad Hasidic sect live. While I found it a rewarding experience, I felt it was an escape from life, not an attempt to come to terms with it.

I met a Tel Aviv man there, a bachelor who liked to have a "good time." He spent his Friday nights at the disco, his Saturdays at the beach. He ate out in good restaurants, traveled abroad, drove a fast car, and did all the things he had dreamed, when he was a struggling student, he would do. Today he found life empty, meaningless, and devoid of content. He had come to Kefar Habad to find out whether there was something more to life than having a good time.

He ate his Friday night supper with a large family. The grand-parents, parents, children, grandchildren, uncles, and cousins sat around the table, singing Sabbath songs, blessing the wine and bread. The following morning he rose early and prayed. Then he had a lesson from one of the Habad elders, which was followed by more praying.

When I met him, late Saturday afternoon, he was overawed. Never, he told me, had he come across such contented people. And it was all without entertainment: no disco, no video, even no television. He had not smoked all day (striking a match to light a cigarette is forbidden to religious Jews on the Sabbath), but he had not felt the need for a cigarette. He had never en-countered such serenity.

Had he found his answer, then? I asked. Was he going to leave it all: the disco, the beach, the girls, the car, the foreign holidays? He shook his head sadly. A part of him wanted to, he told me, but he was too weak.

He might have, though. I never met him again, but — even as I write — he may be praying in some musty shul or learning in a dim *bet midrash* school.

Many have become *ba'alei tshuva* (repentant Jews). One of Is-rael's most famous entertainers, Uri Zohar, a sparkling, talented film actor and director, now has a beard to his waist and dresses in a wide-brimmed hat and black suit with long jacket. That is Uri's answer to the age of the computer and the spaceship: to don seventeenth-century Polish clothes and pore over medieval texts.

We should not forget the ugly, reactionary side of religion: the oppression of women, the fanatical narrow-minded intolerance. Most rabbis tell a battered wife that she is obligated to return to her husband. The young war widow who wishes to remarry is compelled to obtain a release from the brother of her late husband, which can take years if he is too young or if he does not choose to give her a release: years during which the young woman can shrivel up inside. A loving couple is prevented from marrying because one is a Cohen (descended from priests) and the other is a divorcée. Stones are thrown at people who have the temerity to drive on the Sabbath — sometimes even at doctors who have to treat patients.

I can understand a sensitive person who, revolted by the cruelty and immorality of much of modern life, wants to seek refuge in a purer, cleaner past, but we cannot forget about computers and television any more than we can *un*invent the microchip or the nuclear bomb. Furthermore, progress has not been only in a negative direction; science has not been exclusively involved with weapons of destruction.

The blind, the deaf, and the mentally handicapped, who were once locked away in institutions, are now treated in a far more enlightened manner. Only a few years ago, a child with dyslexia could be locked up in a home for the mentally retarded. Today we know that many learning problems are not connected with inherent intelligence. Amazing research is being conducted to help such people.

Wonderful machines have been and are being invented to assist the blind to "see" and the deaf to hear. It is no longer assumed that a deaf child cannot learn to speak. Electronically controlled wheelchairs and ever more sophisticated artificial limbs have given new mobility to the lame.

We have gone past racial and national equality toward respect for the rights of any individual, no matter what his or her handicap. Our new morality must aim at allowing every human being to come into his or her own, to function, to contribute, to gain satisfaction.

Criminals, even murderers, are being rehabilitated rather than punished. It has become fashionable to sneer at psychology and psychiatry, but many have been helped by these new sciences.

Surely morality is what religion is all about — not the breeding of large families to guarantee our claim to a few arid mountains. Surely it is more important to extend the scope of humanity and compassion than to rebuild an ancient Temple and restore animal sacrifices.

Morality can be extended beyond humanity, to every living thing. Animals, too, must be cared for, and I would welcome the abolition of battery-bred poultry and force-fed calves. I doubt that one can go to the extreme in this field. Humanity cannot afford to extend the right of life to the locust; perhaps we should become vegetarians. Of course, there are those who argue that even plants have feelings, so maybe we should synthesize our food. The wonderful thing is that there are no limits. Humankind can advance forever; it does not have to go backward.

We can bring forward the good things from our past traditions. There is much that is valuable in Judaism which I would like to see preserved. The Sabbath is a wonderful idea, even in this era of the thirty-five-hour week and the two-day weekend.

Now, more than ever before, we need a day for rest, repose, and reflection, a day free of the noise of engines and electronic sound, a day liberated from flashing lights and colorful screens, from the rush, bustle, and sheer pressure of modern living. We will benefit from a Sabbath for reading and conversation, for meditation and prayer. But it must come about through education and understanding, not legislation and compulsion. The approach must be positive, not negative; affirmative, not denying.

Today we are in a transition phase, which will last no more than a hundred years and perhaps as few as fifty. The future is catching up with us very quickly indeed. I see it in my own children. Etan is learning computer science to assist him in his chosen career of agricultural engineering. Fourteen-year-old Assaf is growing up with computers, which are a natural part of his life. By the time he is adult, he will surely be punching into computerized information banks as naturally as I scan the advertisement columns of the newspapers, and these information banks will be as easily available to the citizens of Syria or Saudi Arabia as they are to him. Sealed borders will be technically nonexistent.

He and his friends already watch the same television programs and video pop songs that the children across the border watch.

Yariv, the soldier-son of friends of ours, met a wounded Syrian soldier who was being treated in an Israeli hospital. After their initial suspicion, they managed to communicate and found that they had two things in common: a hatred of war and a love of pop music.

The new sounds and their visual expression are international. A British pop group goes to Sri Lanka to make a videotape and an American group films in the Caribbean. One world has already arrived.

My good friend Abu-Shilbaye does not agree with me. He points to history: Muhammad unified the Middle East, but the region later slipped back into individual nations. The Russians conquered Eastern Europe, but Polish nationalism is more alive than ever. "There will always be nations," he tells me, "even in a million years."

But there has never been a time like the present. With the whole wide world open to them, the youth of today put on their jeans, sandals, and beads, grow their hair, hoist their colored rucksacks on their backs, and set off. The young Israelis and Arabs have also started to do it, and it is only a question of time before the young Syrians hike through Israel and the young Israelis through Syria.

In the south it has already started to happen. It is easier for an Israeli to go to Egypt than to many other countries. With your passport and a translated copy of your vehicle license, you can drive across the border into Egyptian Sinai, with only the Egyptian zeal for filling out forms causing a slight delay.

When we crossed the border at Taba, south of Elat, we found the experience exhilarating. The young customs and immigration officials at the border were so open and friendly that the hour and a half consumed by completing forms was also utilized for exchanging addresses in Cairo, El-Arish, Jerusalem, and Galilee and invitations to visit each other's homes.

Later, when we were camping on the wonderful Sinai shore, between the red granite mountains and the fish-filled aquamarine sea, those Egyptian officials came to pay us a visit. We drank coffee and took photographs together, and played backgammon, a popular game in Egypt and Israel. The atmosphere was one of friendship — even warmth. Although the Israel-Egypt peace process is in a deep freeze because of the war in Lebanon and the lack of progress in the West Bank, a half-hour in Sinai dramatically showed us how quickly and easily it can thaw out.

The gun was exchanged for the backgammon board. That is the future: understanding, laughter, comradeship — not the bleak, dark vision of everlasting conflict.

In time the vastness of space and the challenge of other worlds will open up. With his mind on these wider horizons, the citizen of tomorrow will not be obsessed with either Israel or Palestine. Plumbing the depths of the ocean, reaching the stars, finding the secrets of the human mind, discovering more about the structure of matter, creating new forms of art and culture — these are the tasks and challenges that will occupy our grandchildren, if only we manage to bequeath them a world and not a smoking cemetery.

Meanwhile, we in this century are charged with the more prosaic task of bridging the gap, of preparing the ground, of making sure that our world does not blow itself up before it can start achieving its limitless potential.

We here in Israel and our neighbors in the Middle East must ensure that we become a laboratory for coexistence and cooperation and not a tinderbox for Armageddon. We must seize the initiative from the forces of darkness and repression on both sides of the border.

We in Israel, who have fought so hard and so bitterly for our national independence, must be the first to say, "No piece of land, no stone, no Temple is worth the sacrifice of human life."

That is why we must be prepared to repartition our ancient homeland. No doubt, if we hang on and fight, we can have all the Land of Israel for ourselves, but at what cost? Let us give up what we think is rightly ours, let us take risks in order to save lives.

Was the capture of the Beaufort Castle worth it? Did it merit the lives of Guni Harnik, Yaron Zamir, and their fellows? Let us recall for an instant the terrible grief of Rama and Yehoshua Zamir. Let us remember the laughing, vital Yaron, who gave warmth and friendship to his family and friends, who comforted the bereaved girl of his friend Yaniv. Let us remember Yaron, who was raised with love beneath the shadow of Mount Tabor. Let us multiply him by hundreds, by thousands, and let us resolve: never again.

It may be that we will have to fight again to defend ourselves, but never again must war be used when there is an alternative way. Never again must war be an instrument of policy.

In our country and in the world at large, the real battle must be joined. It is the battle between love and hatred, light and darkness — between the soldier who would not cry for his dead sister and the soldier who cries when he watches "Little House on the Prairie."

Let us then jettison our surplus baggage, let us gather up the good in our past, let us hitch our rucksacks onto our backs and take the first, faltering step forward. This is our challenge, our charge, our privilege.